SELMA

Swedish Fortitude on the North Dakota Frontier

Lela Selma Peterson

WOODSON BOOKS

Published by WOODSON BOOKS
1420 Eagle Avenue
Reynolds, North Dakota USA

ISBN 978-1514320358

Front cover of photo Selma and Johan Sjöqvist, 1895.

Book design by LaVonne Ewing, great-granddaughter of Selma.

Scripture quotations from The Holy Bible, New International Version, 1973, 1984; International Bible Society.

DEDICATION

In loving memory of my grandmother,
Selma Amanda Dahlgren Sjöqvist.
She will be a model for our family
for all future generations.

*"Many women do noble things, but you surpass
them all. Charm is deceptive, and beauty is fleeting;
but a woman who fears the LORD is to be praised."*
Proverbs 31:29-30

CONTENTS

MAJOR CHANGES

MAGNET TO THE WEST

LIVES OF CHILDREN

APPENDIX

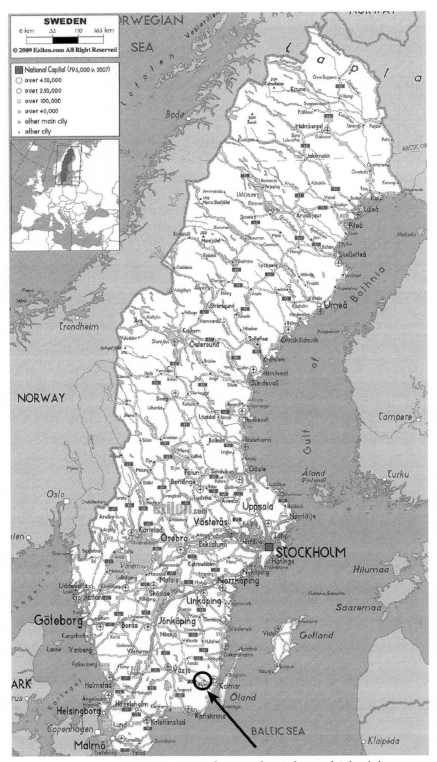

Nybro, Sweden; Selma and Johan's home area

SWEDISH WORDS & PLACES

Adjö - (formal) good-bye

Algustboda - where the Hultqvist family lived and where Ester worked

Ära Vara Gud - to God be the Glory

Ariosto - boat taking Johan from Göteborg, Sweden to Hull, England

Calypso - boat taking Selma and children from Göteborg, Sweden to Hull, England

Ellis Island, New York - where new immigrants were processed into the United States

Far - father

Farfar - father's father

Farmor - father's mother

Göteborg - seaport city on the west coast where Selma and Johan left Sweden

Gränö - location of a cluster of homes where Selma and Johan lived

Hej då - good-bye

Hultqvist - family in Algustboda where Ester worked

Ja - yes

Krona - means crown, term for Swedish money

Kyrkotagning - prayer of thanksgiving, introduction of mother into church after birth

Län - county

Lysning - for three weeks prior to a wedding the pastor announces the upcoming marriage and asks for any objections

Madesjö - Lutheran Church of Nybro

Många tack - many thanks

Midsummar - middle of summer, a special holiday

Min älskade - My beloved

Mor - mother

Morfar - mother's father (grandfather)

Mormor - mother's mother (grandmother)

Nej - no

Nybro - nearest town to Selma and Johan's Swedish home

Sillgatan Street - also known as Postgatan in city of Göteborg (where tickets were purchased to America)

Småland - southeast province where the family lived

S. S. Kristianiafjord - steamship that Ester & Erik sailed on (Bergen, Norway to New York)

S. S. Saxonia - steamship that Selma & Johan sailed on (Liverpool to Boston)

Sverige - Sweden

Tack - thank you

Tjukehall - place where Johan grew up

Utffyttningsbok - parish records of people going out (leaving)

Västergötland - a province in western Sweden

FAMILY TREE

Selma's Parents
Maria Helena Jonsson
 b. July 7, 1831
 † Oct. 3, 1913

  m. Oct. 7, 1868

Johan Dahlgren
 b. June 4, 1829
 † Jan. 8, 1914

Johan's Parents
Christina Petersdotter
 b. Dec. 3, 1837
 † Mar 24, 1908

  m. Nov. 3, 1868

Frans Peter Olsson Sjögren
 b. Dec. 9, 1838
 † Jan. 18, 1901

Selma Amanda
 b. Apr. 25, 1870
 USA Oct. 18, 1904
 † Aug. 21, 1961
 no siblings

  m. Feb. 19, 1895

Johan Alfred Sjöqvist
 b. Apr. 4, 1869
 USA Mar. 13, 1903
 † Oct. 3, 1911

Selma & Johan's Children
Ester Gunhild Alfrida
 b. Dec. 1, 1895
 USA Jan. 23, 1915
 † Apr. 6, 1954

Herman Gunnar Emanuel
 b. Nov. 14, 1896
 USA Oct. 18, 1904
 † Feb. 16, 1969

John Ragnar Julius
 b. June 16, 1898
 USA Oct. 18, 1904
 † Aug. 8, 1970

Ingeborg Ragnhild Eleonora
 b. July 12, 1901
 USA Oct. 18, 1904
 † Dec. 27, 1973

Erik Knut Valdemar
 b. May 31, 1903
 USA Jan. 23, 1915
 † July 20, 1966

Ruth Josefina Helena
 b. Aug. 10, 1905
 † Mar. 29, 1974

Edwin Sigmund Herbert
 b. May 6, 1907
 † Apr. 22, 1915

Johan's Siblings
Hulda Sophia
 b. Mar. 25, 1871
 † Mar. 8, 1891

Carl Wilhelm
 b. July 31, 1873
 † Nov. 14, 1876

Pehr Olof
 b. Feb. 12, 1876
 † May 17, 1903

Alma Augusta
 b. Feb. 12, 1879
 † Dec. 5, 1966

Carl Wilhelm
 b. May 16, 1882
 † May 8, 1894

SJÖGREN - "branch"
SJÖQVIST - "twig"

b. date of birth
m. date of marriage
USA date of leaving Sweden
† date of death

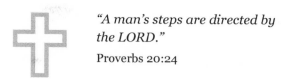

"A man's steps are directed by the LORD."
Proverbs 20:24

Introduction

In writing about my grandparents, mother, aunts, and uncles I have come to a clearer understanding of myself. This surprised me. Never in my wildest dreams did I ever think this was possible.

Maybe the statement by Seth Godin is true: "Here's the thing: The book that will most change your life is the book you write." This was certainly the case for me.

Through my journey I have come to respect and appreciate all the hardships my grandparents went through. They came to North Dakota for a better way of life. They never returned to their beloved homeland and therefore never, ever saw Sweden again.

My grandparents planned to make their fortunes in one year and return. All this changed upon arrival. During their life in North Dakota, they endured difficulties that I find impossible to wrap my thoughts around. I often wonder, if they had known what lay before them, would they have come?

With each hurdle Selma and Johan appeared to hang onto each other more deeply in love. They were strengthened with a fierce determination that they would make it with the help of their faith in Almighty God.

My grandparents were pioneers in the truest sense of the word. They instilled the value of hard work and a desire to succeed regardless of the adversities flung into their paths. They wanted to have a better life for their children and grandchildren.

And, this is where it hits close to home. As their grandchild, I have had opportunities unfold in front of me that even my parents would find unbelievable. My grandparents would be aghast of all the modern conveniences that are at my everyday disposal. These are all possible because of the sacrifices they made.

I knew my grandmother and six of her seven adult children. But, I did not know them well. As a child I remembered visiting my Mormor (grandma). Although the times were few and far between, I adored her quiet, deep nature. She taught me to count and say a few words in Swedish. When she came for a visit I sat mesmerized and entranced as I listened to the Swedish conversations among neighbors and her own adult children. I deeply yearned to know, to understand, and to love her more.

As I researched my grandparents and their children, each of them took on personal characteristics. Unique to themselves. I came to feel for them in a way that was so profound, it shocked my inner being. As I read of them, I cried over their downfalls and failures. But, I also rejoiced and laughed with their successes. In my eyes they were no longer just names, but people that I walked beside, thought of while having my tea, and had dreams of.

What I'm trying to say, is that each person became a real, live human being. I drew deeply from the past stories my mother had shared with me. I wrote them the way I remembered her words. They remain one of my most priceless treasures.

I did take liberty as a writer to add dialogue. This was used to bring about an understanding of a particular situation. In doing so, I have attempted to respect the people involved. It was only done after much prayerful thought.

By my research and writing, I have been given untold blessings. When meeting roadblocks, I would stop for a period of time and then after feeling restored I persevered. My motto became: "How can I know where I'm going, unless I know where I've come from."

My admiration for my forefathers has been deepened. My grandmother, Selma Amanda Dahlgren Sjöqvist, is a woman that I not only revere, but I try to emulate. She was one of a kind. In some small way (other than my own middle name) if I can come to be more like her, I would truly be blessed.

I once read, "Looking back is how we best see God in action." How true, how true!

Ära Vara Gud!!   To God be the Glory!!
Lela Selma

EARLY DAYS

"And now these three remain: faith, hope and love. But the greatest of these is love."

1 Corinthians 13:13

The Kyrkotagning

August 18, 1901

P astor Medelius was surprised when Selma requested a prayer of thanksgiving. The *kyrkotagning*, a very old church custom dating back to early Christian days, was rarely done anymore. It was an act of gratitude and a way for Selma to be welcomed back into the church after the birth of her daughter. She told the pastor she wanted to come forward and publicly thank God. Pastor Medelius thought, "Selma's request certainly is unusual! She must be a woman of great faith."

Madesjö Lutheran Church of Nybro, Sweden (2010)

℘ THE MORNING LIGHT STREAMED through the windows of the huge and majestic building in Madesjö, Sweden. It fell on the rose granite baptismal font at the front of the Lutheran church.

Selma knew she needed to pay close attention to what was happening, but her mind drifted. Selma had always wanted a large family. Maybe it was the result of being raised as an only child in Johan and Maria Dahlgren's household. Or maybe it was her deep love for her husband Johan Sjöquist. Whatever the reason, jointly they shared a strong desire for children. Lots of them.

And so she thought of the baby in her arms, her fourth child, a beautiful little girl. Her daughter. A month earlier at the same baptismal font that now shone in the brilliance of the morning sun had been the christening of Ingeborg Ragnhild Eleonora by Pastor Medelius, a daughter born July 12th. At her baptism she had only been three days old.

Selma looked down at her newborn baby and maternal love poured from her deepest being. She didn't relish standing and speaking in front of people, but she had such a strong desire to publicly thank God for this little bundle in her arms.

Before Selma could gather her thoughts, the pastor beckoned her to come forward. It was time for her *kyrkotagning*. Selma slowly rose from the pew where the entire family was seated. She stuffed all fears aside and walked to the front of the church with baby Ingeborg in her arms.

She held her head high until she approached the front of the church. Stopping for a few seconds she bowed her head and knelt before the altar. Looking down once again at her infant daughter, her words came easily. She forgot all the rehearsed thoughts she had practiced over and over in her mind. Instead she spoke from deep within her heart.

Baptismal font dating from 1655

"God, I thank and praise you, for a healthy child. Together Johan and I have given life to our love in the form of a baby girl. Only you, O Lord, could make this possible. You are a wonderful, loving God." She continued to express her gratefulness that she and her husband had been blessed once again.

By the time she finished Selma was unable to utter another word. She

Kyrkoherde (Pastor) J. O. Medelius
(1844 - 1911) served Selma and Johan
in Sweden.

had choked back so many tears and yet she kept herself under control and made it to the very end.

Selma arose. Pastor Medelius clasped her hand while bestowing the blessing on her. "The Lord guide you in His truth and fear, now and unto eternity. Amen."

Her eyes scanned the congregation and finally landed on her husband. Johan's deep blue eyes penetrated through her and shone with admiration and love. But it was his small, ever so slight, smile that gave her the courage she needed. Oh, how she loved this man. Her husband.

Walking slowly back to her family pew, she slipped into her spot by Johan. She felt him squeeze her hand. It was only then the tears silently fell down her cheeks. There was no holding them back. Her heart was filled to overflowing. ∽

Church Altar (2010)

"Be joyful always; pray continually; give thanks in all circumstances, for this is God's will for you in Christ Jesus."

1 Thessalonians 5:16

Tough Times

1895-1903

Selma dreamed of one day having space. Room to work and lots of room for children to play freely. But such was not the case today. Space was at a premium in the 15- x 25-foot cottage in Gränö. Selma, Johan, and their four children squeezed into a small two-room dwelling. They had been financially forced to move and live with Selma's parents, Johan and Maria Dahlgren. Selma was so grateful these dear people had opened their hearts and home to welcome her family. She also realized this wasn't easy for them, but they never grumbled or complained.

Road Sign for Gränö (2010)

Gränö was a small settlement of homes clustered close together. The Dahlgren's cottage was on the outside edge of all the others. A large grassy meadow surrounded the home, and the area was bordered by countless birch and evergreen trees, offering both shade and sunshine. It was also a buffer zone from their neighbors.

The house was small *before* Selma and Johan moved in. Their move now added six more people to the mix. Altogether, this made for a tight, close family. People were always stepping over or tripping on one another.

⁊ AS SELMA COOKED AND CLEANED, her mind often wandered. She thought of the time when she was only 25 and had been courted by a dashing six-foot-two, blue-eyed, and brown-haired Swede from Tjukehall, Johan

Alfred Sjöqvist. He was 26 years old and lived only a short distance down the road. His family name was Sjögren (meaning "branch"), but Johan wanted something different. Thus, he chose the last name of Sjöqvist (meaning "twig").

When Selma accepted Johan's proposal of marriage, the two requested a *lysning* in the church. For three weeks prior to their wedding, Pastor Medelius announced each Sunday their upcoming marriage and asked if there were any objections. Each time the announcement was made, Selma had numerous mixed emotions. She wavered from dread of objection to happy anticipation of the upcoming marriage. But she had nothing to fear. The only comments ever made occurred after the service and all were positive.

Selma would never, ever forget their wedding on February 19, 1895. It was truly a dream come true. She wore a dark, floor length dress with a contrasting stark white, ruffled collar. White ruffles overlaid the front of her bodice, and the long sleeves had an overlay of a dark cape and ended in white ruffles at the wrist. It wasn't her dress, white gloves, or flowers she carried that made her feel like a bride. It was the long, floor length veil that hung from the fabric flowers in her hair.

Wedding picture of Selma and Johan Sjöqvist, February 19, 1895. *Photo: Hedvig Rosendahl, Stockholm, Sweden*

Selma's "prince" stood beside her wearing a black, three-piece suit. His white gloves, starched white shirt and bowtie accented his slender body. Johan wore his light brown hair short and parted slightly off to the right side, but he had a moustache that was above all moustaches. As Selma glanced over at him, she had to stifle a small giggle that wanted to erupt from her nervous body. Between his nose and upper lip was the largest dark brown triangle of hair, she'd ever seen on her love. She sobered herself when she saw the seriousness of Johan's erect body. Immediately, she knew he was nervous and laughing would be extremely inappropriate. ∞

Madesjö Lutheran Church Altar of Nybro, Sweden (1967)

ᔅᔆᔆ WHEN LITTLE INGEBORG CRIED, Selma stopped all thoughts of the past and her focus returned to the needs of her little one.

Besides the larger bodies struggling for work space, there were four youngsters who wanted to play and partake in more rambunctious activities. Therefore, Selma often sent six-year-old Ester outside to watch over her two younger brothers, Herman and John. Soon their baby sister, Ingeborg, would be big enough to join them. The children spent countless hours together playing in the dirt and tall grass. They piled up rocks and stones and built things with twigs and branches.

The one thing that Selma knew her family all shared was an abundance of love. The grandparents doted over the four little ones. Mormor often took the children out into the fields and countryside in search of berries while Morfar occupied them with bits of scrap leather and laces.

Both Selma's father Johan and husband Johan were shoemakers. To her it seemed ironic that both of these men whom she loved not only shared the same name of Johan, but also similar trades. In spite of two shoemakers living in one household, the children often ran barefoot. The soles of their feet were like leather. Their Far had explained that the bigger pieces of precious leather were needed to make shoes that could be sold. The family needed money more than Johan's own children needed shoes.

But, how many shoes can a shoemaker repair or make in one small vil-

lage? And to think that these two men were attempting to support themselves and those they loved. With other shoemakers close by, it became difficult if not impossible.

Times became very tough for this little family. Money was tight and eight people from two families were cramped together in one very, very small house. Something had to be done. They were at their breaking point. ⮿

Remains of Dahlgren
Home (1967)

Ulla-Britt Johansson
(2010)

Ragnar and Hildur Johansson with Lela in the middle (June 1967)

Note: Ragnar was the son of Karl and Anna Johansson and as an adult lived with his wife Hildur in the home of his parents. They were the closest neighbors of the Dahlgren/Sjöqvist family. They often spoke of the crowded living conditions in the very small home of the Dahlgren's.

In 2010 Ulla-Britt Johansson, daughter of Ragnar and Hildur, lived in the home formerly owned by Karl & Anna (grandparents) and Ragnar & Hildur (parents). She lived here in the summer and spent winters in Göteborg. And so, this home remains in the Johansson family.

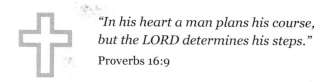

"In his heart a man plans his course, but the LORD determines his steps."

Proverbs 16:9

Quandary

1900 - 1903

One winter day Johan heard of a way out of his severe money crunch. Advertisements were posted everywhere and included in every Sverige newspaper. "Come to America. The land is free. Throw the wheat into the soil and become rich in one year. Gold awaits those that come."

Advertising promoted settlement and homesteading. Railroads, land agencies, the Dakota territory, and later the state of North Dakota carried on large commercial campaigns. Everyone would benefit. Increased population would mean more railroad freight and passengers. Greater land values would benefit land agents and add increased revenue for the government.

"Could it be so easy?" Johan wondered as he looked again at an ad. "Reports of forty bushels to the acre wheat crop with wheat selling for $1.25 a bushel. If it is as grand as we are told, maybe I should give it a try."

Talk around the community ran wild about the number of young people leaving the local area for America. In addition to all the propaganda and gossip, Johan had received letters from his friends in America. Carl and Aron Johansson, plus their father Ole, had emigrated to North Dakota. Ole had left in 1886 and his sons in 1896. Johan felt the tug of free land. But, it required a willingness to cross the gigantic Atlantic Ocean.

Johan realized his own family was enlarging in number. Making and repairing shoes provided a meager income. He had tried to plant a crop on the little plot of ground surrounding their cottage. Repeated crop failures were making it increasingly difficult to make a living even with the combined income of shoemaking and a crop from the tiny land plot.

The rural conditions were especially bleak in the Småland province where the family resided. This southern region had become the heartland of emigration from Sweden. Between 1.3 and 1.4 million people out of 5.5 million (more than one-fifth of the entire population of the region) left during the late 1800s and early 1900s. Each passing day Johan and Selma learned of more young people leaving the area.

He and Selma whispered the pros and cons late into the night, but Johan lay awake as he pondered what he should do. If he remained in Sweden, would things improve? He desperately wanted to provide for his growing family. He wanted to be independent and stop leaning on Selma's parents. The Dahlgrens were not the reason for him to leave. They were wonderful people and never, ever complained. But, the more he evaluated each aspect of the depressed Swedish economy against the needs of his children, there was only one answer. He needed to go! ∞

A railroad advertisement for free land in Central Dakota

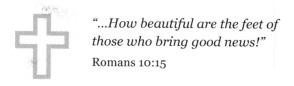

"...How beautiful are the feet of those who bring good news!"

Romans 10:15

The Letter

Early in 1902

Johan dropped the letter that was in his hand to the kitchen table. He couldn't believe what he had just read. Could it be possible? Could he be so fortunate?

He lifted his eyes to find Selma staring at him. Johan knew his wife well enough to know that she desperately wanted to understand the expression reflected on his face. With a few quick steps, Johan grabbed Selma in his arms and swung her around the small cottage.

"What is it, Johan? What does your letter say to make you so happy? Please tell me." Selma eagerly wanted to share in whatever news Johan had received.

"Sit down, my Selma. This is the best news ever. I just can't believe it."

Selma sat and patiently waited for her husband to read the lengthy letter. He wanted to read it hastily, but forced himself to read it at a slower pace so Selma would be able to grasp the true meaning.

Dear Johan,

This is Aron Johnson, your long lost Swedish friend from North Dakota. I don't know where to begin to tell you the wonderful news that I have to share.

I got married on November 30, 1901 to a most beautiful Norwegian gal, named Nora Knutson. Her father, mother, brother, and other youngsters arrived here earlier this year from Freeborn, Minnesota.

Nora had filed all the paperwork for her very own homestead. In fact the paperwork had only been completed by the end of October. This parcel of land lays directly to the east of my claim. In order to prove Nora's claim, she would need to remain as head of the household and consistently reside there.

In other words, one of us needs to relinquish our claim, because we can't be married and also the head of our own home on separate claims. Because I have mine established and hers is brand new, we plan to release her 160 acre homestead claim.

If we kept it until you got here - would you want it? Just think, Johan, 160 acres could be yours free for the taking.

If you do want it, you will need to come as quickly as possible. It would probably be too soon for you to make it this year in 1902, but do you think you could make it early in the spring of 1903? I think we can hold it until then.

Give my love to your wife and children. I'm certain they are all getting big. Pray hard about this (and then come).

Waiting to hear from you,

Aron and Nora Johnson

By the way, Nora's younger brother, Joseph, is always eager to help others. He has helped me out a number of times and I know he'd do the same by you. Joseph is too young to take Nora's claim. So don't worry about that. ∽

Aron and Nora Johnson
(late 1901 or 1902)

"...take note of this:
Everyone should be quick
to listen, slow to speak..."
James 1:19

Selma's Reaction

Early in 1902

Selma looked at her husband. His face radiated joy, love, and excitement. Looking into his deep blue eyes, she smiled. Her happiness was neither deep nor profound like his. Immediately Johan recognized that Selma was holding something back, for her smile never reached her eyes.

"What is it, my love? Do you not see the opportunities that have been opened to us?"

Selma cast her eyes downward as she contemplated her answer. She didn't want to put a wet blanket on her husband's joy. "Yes, Johan, I do see this as a wonderful offer. It is really remarkable. I cannot fathom the two of us owning 160 acres."

"Then tell me, why do you hesitate so?"

"Johan, please understand, what I am about to say. You must remember that I am an only child. My parents have only me, you, and the children. It will break their hearts if we all leave at once." Selma looked up at this sweet, dear man she loved. "I want you to go. But, maybe I should stay awhile here and come later. Then Mor and Far would get used to the idea. This is not what I want, but it would be a compromise. What do you think?"

Then Selma added a question that Johan had never contemplated. "Would we only stay until we gathered our own wealth? Would we come back home after that?"

Taking Selma's hands in his own calloused large ones, Johan rubbed his thumbs on the backs of her hands. He looked past her as he thought deeply about her comments. After a few minutes, he searched her eyes, "Ja, Selma, I suppose you are right. It will be hard to leave you and the children, but maybe it would be best. I'd need to have a place for you to live and I'd need to build that. You know, I do believe that would be a good thing. And in answer to your last questions, of course if we got rich, there would be no reason that we couldn't or wouldn't come back."

Standing up, Johan pulled his wife to her feet. "You've always been the practical one. That's one of the reasons I love you so." Putting his arms around her he hugged his Selma.

"Now comes the hard part. Let's go tell your folks. It is a wonderful thing, Selma. I just pray they'll see it that way." Taking Selma's hand, the young couple strolled out to the meadow where the grandparents sat watching the little children as they played. ⚭

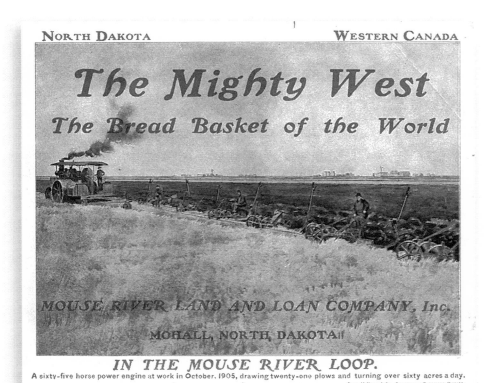

An advertisement for land in the Mouse River Loop depicting 21 plows turning over 60 acres a day (1905)

"Blessed is the man who perseveres under trial, because when he has stood the test, he will receive the crown of life that God has promised to those who love him."

James 1:12

Mixed Blessings

1902 - 1903

Mormor and Morfar looked up and watched as their daughter and her husband walked towards them. Mormor's heart began to beat a little faster. It was the mixed emotions she read on Selma's face that concerned her. Her daughter looked down as the two walked. Johan, on the other hand, had an expression of undeniable excitement and joy. He was beaming until they noticed he glanced in Selma's direction. Instantly, Johan mirrored some of Selma's worry.

Morfar stood and waved to the couple as they approached. "Come see the game your children have made up all by themselves. They are very creative little ones."

Selma's eyes didn't meet her father's, but she put a shallow smile on her face as she looked up.

"What is it, Selma? You have the look of concern on your face." Mormor looked from Morfar to Selma. "Don't be afraid to tell us whatever you have on your mind."

Selma looked directly at her mother and then searched her father's eyes. "Well, you see, Johan has received a letter from his friend, Aron Johnson, in America. Do you remember him? He grew up in our church parish."

Johan looked from his mother-in-law to his father-in-law. "There's really no easy way to tell you what Aron said. But, there is a homestead claim available next to Aron's that I can get for free in North Dakota. It would be 160 acres. It is a once-in-a-lifetime opportunity."

Selma watched as her parents looked at each other. Tears came quickly to her mother's eyes, but her father's eyes held lots of questions. "Will you go too, my daughter?"

"No, I'd wait and let Johan check it all out. He needs to prepare for me and the children to come. It would take him a while to do all that." Selma could easily see her response gave her parents comfort. They even tried to smile, but it was really only half-hearted and Selma immediately recognized it for what it was. They knew that down the road they would still be facing farewells with this daughter they held such intense love for.

Johan added, almost as an afterthought, "If we can acquire enough wealth, Selma and I will return as soon as possible. It shouldn't take too long, I wouldn't think."

Morfar shook Johan's hand in a gesture of congratulations. "I really do wish you well. It is especially good that you will check it out first by yourself. Before your wife and children."

Mormor searched Johan's face. With worry lines on her brow she ventured, "And when will you leave? We must prepare for it so you are ready."

"Well, I really doubt that I can be ready to leave until next year. I'll need to save every penny in order to buy the ticket. I'll need some cash to bring as well." Johan paused. He reached for Selma's hand. "The thing we need the most is your blessing. What do you think?" ᣠ

Selma and Johan (1902 or 1903)
Photo: Richard Blomdahl, Stockholm, Sweden

"Now faith is being sure of what we hope for and certain of what we do not see."

Hebrews 11:1

Leaving and Arriving

1903 - 1904

And so it was, on March 13, 1903, Johan prepared to leave his family in Gränö. Saying "good-bye" to Selma was excruciatingly painful. They had talked many hours about his leaving, but doing it was another matter. As Johan held Selma in a tight embrace, he felt her swollen abdomen. They both laughed when the baby she carried within her gave a resounding kick. Johan felt it and immediately stepped back. "Wow! That little one really wants me to get going! By the feel of the baby's jab, it must be a boy!!"

"We'll see. Only a couple more months and we'll know for sure." Selma tried hard to mask her feelings. As she waved farewell to Johan, she felt like someone had just squeezed her so tight that she would never ever be able to breathe again.

The *Ariosto* carried Johan from Sweden to England.

With tears running down his cheeks and trepidation in his heart, Johan turned to leave.

℘ HE SET OFF BY TRAIN for the western coast of southern Sweden. The port city of Göteborg was Johan's first destination. Here tickets needed to be purchased for the entire journey. After doing this, he located the Emigration Building at the city's harbor and proceeded with necessary paperwork. On the next leg of the journey, he would sail and stay overnight in Hull, England. Then he would take a train to Liverpool. After another night or two in Liverpool, Johan would finally sail to America.

On board the vessel *Saxonia*, Johan reclaimed his original excitement. This huge steamer ship was capable of carrying over 2,000 people with 1,600 being third class. Third class or "draft" or "steerage" was the most affordable way Johan found for his passage to the New Country. Being crowded on the lower deck was somewhat familiar. It reminded him of his tight quarters at the old home in Gränö.

"Things have to be better in this new land to the west," he thought. "I can do this. I know I can."

Johan spent most of his time on deck. It didn't take long to realize that he wanted to spend as little time as possible in the steerage area. It was just too dark and dismal on the lower level. Smells were suffocating and people were packed in tight as they sat and laid all over the floors.

He was heading for the port of Boston with his final destination being Kenmare, North Dakota by way of Estevan, Saskatchewan in Canada. He

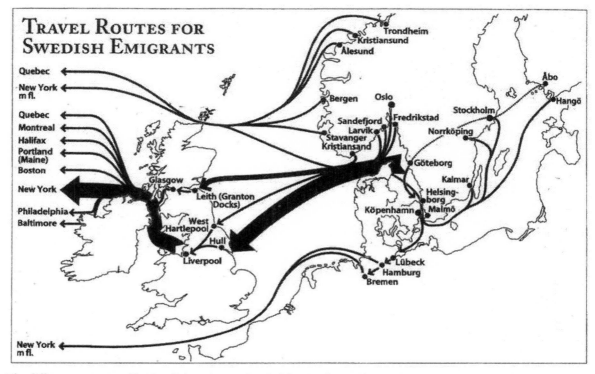

The different routes used by Swedish emigrants headed for North America.

knew very little of this new land in front of him. He carried no luggage, so he had absolutely no fears of having to protect worldly possessions. The ten dollars in his pocket would allow him limited resources. But, the one thing Johan had was an abundance of hopes and dreams.

Johan traveled from Liverpool, England across the ocean on the *S. S. Saxonia*, as did Selma, Herman, John and Ingeborg on a later voyage.

℘ JOHAN COULDN'T BELIEVE the wide expanse of the Atlantic Ocean. On April 3, Boston was on the horizon. He had made it.

First- and second-class passengers were checked by immigration officials on board and allowed to directly leave the *Saxonia*. All third-class passengers were sent through more rigorous scrutiny by the officials. From the steamer, they were taken into the Boston Customs Building for immigration inspection.

After what seemed like hours, Johan was cleared to leave. For the price of one dollar he boarded a train for his journey halfway across the United States and Canada. After watching for hours out the window, he realized the vastness of this land. He never expected America to be so immense. By the time he arrived in North Dakota his eagerness had ebbed somewhat from the weariness of travel.

Surveying his homestead, Johan stood at the top of a hill and gazed in disbelief at what lay before him…160 acres. It measured one half mile square. Until he actually laid eyes on his land he had found it difficult to perceive the vastness. As he shaded his eyes he noticed coulees to the northeast, rolling land to the southeast, a river to the west, and between it all beautiful flat land. Johan found it overwhelming. He would need to do a lot of work to conquer this large untamed chunk of land. Wow! And to think it would all be his one day.

Johan was surprised when he learned of the large number of people homesteading in North Dakota. Many in the Mouse River Valley area spoke Swedish. It felt good to be understood in his native tongue.

Johan was eager to find the Johansson brothers. They had Americanized their names. Aron, like his father, had taken the last name of Johnson. Carl had chosen a different spelling with the name of Jonson. They were naturalized American citizens now.

Johan became a neighbor to both the Johansson brothers. Aron lived to the west and Carl to the south. These two were slowly changing from raising cattle to general grain farming. In the early years before homesteading was opened up, the brothers had enjoyed raising cattle on an open range. But times were changing, fences were going up and ranchers were quickly becoming farmers.

Through the remainder of 1903 and 1904 Johan relied heavily on Carl, Aron, and others for help. There was so much to do. In the back of his mind Johan questioned the dream of returning to Sweden with great wealth. The advertisements and wild talk in the Old Country had been stretched far beyond all imagination. If he would ever be able to survive in this new land Johan knew beyond a shadow of a doubt that it would be difficult, backbreaking labor to accomplish everything required of homesteaders.

"Yes, I will do all of this. Then, my Selma can come here and I can see her and the children once more. It will all be worth it." And with these thoughts in mind he focused on the mighty tasks in front of him. ∽

TOWNSHIP 160   **RANGE 86**

Andrew Johnson	Detlet Hansen / Jeanette Johnson	John Slattery	John W. Morris	Frank Trudell	Joseph Trudell	Judd Peterman	Maret Leimon	Susan Dudley	Arthur Dudley	Charles A. Larson	C. McCusick
Helen C. Winnie / M.O. Davis (Ed)	Brer Hanson / Mary L. Ryan		Martin Lyder	William Trockstad	George H. Gorbig	Marion A. Brown	Simon E. Olsen	Carl A. Owenson	Orville R. Walker	Eddy Larson	Benjamin W. McCusick
Charles Bennett Mackey / Martin Bayfield	Ole Syverson		Thomas Forestad	Richard W. Kingdahl	George Fitch	Andrew Attwood	Carl August Olson	John Christianson	Lawrence L. Brinkmann	John Gilbert	Andrew P. Anderson
Boyle	Ole Skilerud / Jans Janson / Peder	John Noonan	John Serveld	Nils Kvale	Micheal Distad	Charles Atwood	Edwin Atwood	Louis Kellersman	Harry A. Wichmann	Charley Dammann	Harry Applelorn
Philip	Ludwig Peterson		Thomas B. Hastings			John A. Swifert	Patrick J. Sullivan	C. Schneiderman	Ras. Johnson	C. Appledorn	Elizabeth Wichmann
	Samuel Dagg / Annie Skilerud / Peter Johnson	John E. Johnson / Eliza A. Sloan				Bert A. Belisle	Albert J. Sankey	Tollef A. Egge	Christina Moora Halvorson	M. Joseph Conway	Stephen V. Conway
Sam A. Hystad	Jens Anderson	Olson	Herman Kolbo	John H. Greer	Daniel Keane	Alfred S. Taute		J.J. Wharley	Andrew F. Wherley	S. Emil Nelson	Leonard P. Peterson
Henry Gullickson	George E. Whiting	Elna / Orlando Frick Johnson	Troen Johnson	Bessie M. Lewis	Helmuth Boerner	Knute T. Roble	William Dowton	Andrew Wherley	Sarah Collins	Elizabeth Cawley	David C. Kridler
Leon D. Torell	Joe A. Stub-Krace	Harry M. Cooke	Aaron Johnson	**Johan Sjöqvist**	George L. Austin	Eliza A. McKintie	H.W. Hely	Eliza B. Manley	Elizabeth Gullakson	S. Hove	Anton Ness
Walter H. Martine	Theodore H. Kolbo	C. Schweitzer	Oscar M. Lindblom / Harry Winsel	Joseph Knutson		William Heinz	J. Custer	Mary A.A. Manley	Gustave Hendrickson	F. Schmidt	Iver E. Olson
John H. Pautz	Joseph Miller	William Shores	Harry Winsel / J.R. Rasmussen	Margaret A. Murphy	Karl Johan Johnson	Peter Nels	William F. Truax	Caroline Hemmott	Margaret A. Murphy	Hans Torgerson	Peter R. Johnson
Amelie Gunelia Marcophtvedt	Paulina E.	Lewis E. Shores	Richard Axtelle	Mary A. Klemmens	Clyde W. Joslin	Lenora Rufsvold	James Armstrong	Nora Tucker	Mary B. Crawford		

Sjöqvist Homestead:
Township 162 (note discrepancy) and Range 86
Section 28
West half of NE quarter & East half of NW quarter

Renville County History 1901–1976, page 337
Renville County Old Settler's Association

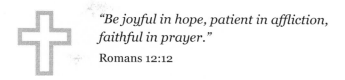

Hopes and Dreams

1903 – 1904

O ne fall day in October 1904 a decision was made. Selma met with the pastor of the Madesjö church. After much deliberation, she came to request her name and three of her five children be released from the church.

This decision weighed heavily on her. The church she attended in Madesjö was in charge of all record keeping for a large region in Småland. Everyone coming into and leaving from the parish came here to register. All her life Selma had been a part of this church. It had been a huge focal point in her life.

On October 18, 1904 Selma, Herman, John, and Ingeborg had their names entered into the Utffyttningsbok. They would be leaving Gränö for North America. Selma knew this was the first of many ties that she needed to sever.

&) WHILE JOHAN WORKED NONSTOP in America, Selma had stayed behind in Gränö with the four youngsters. They ranged in age from seven years old down to little Ingeborg who was not quite two. And soon a baby would be born. With her husband gone, Selma leaned heavily on her loving parents. Without them things would be most difficult.

On May 31, 1903, just two and half months after Johan left Sweden, a son, Erik Knut Valdemar, was born. Selma's joy was overshadowed by the distance between her baby and his father. Erik's older brothers and sisters loved him unconditionally. They wanted to help their Mor in caring for their new baby brother. He was a happy child and adored by everyone.

The warm summer days passed quickly in Sweden and the children continued to grow. Ingeborg's favorite pastime was going with Mormor, Grandma Dahlgren, to pick lingonberries.

Sometimes the lingonberries were found close to their home. At other times they took long walks to locate them. Using her apron, Mormor carefully picked the small red jewels. They were sour to eat freshly picked, but she would sweeten them just right for jams, toppings, and baked goods.

Lingonberry plants grew in the home area.

ᘓ AFTER SELMA COMPLETED HER VISIT with the pastor, she continued to ready herself for departure. Her plan was to help her husband gather the wealth in America and return back to Sweden. With this idea in mind she knew it wouldn't be long until both parents would return to their oldest and youngest children, Ester and baby Erik. Knowing she could help Johan shorten the time, Selma mustered up the strength to leave these two children behind. There was simply not enough money for more tickets. In addition, if all the family were to leave at once, it would simply be too difficult for Selma's parents. She knew Ester and Erik would be well cared for by their loving grandparents. Leaving her children would cushion the fact that she and the others would be so very far away. Selma cautioned herself about worry and fretting. After all, it wouldn't be long and they would all soon return to their beloved Old Country. Hopefully, richer!

Johan had thought of everything to make Selma's trip as easy as possible. Amongst his North Dakota friends, it was decided that Carl, the youngest of the Johansson brothers at age 26 would leave his North Dakota homestead and return to Sweden. He was to assist Selma and the three children on their journey. He brought enough money to pay for all four of their passageways.

With Carl's able assistance Selma relaxed somewhat. He explained each and every leg of the journey and what was about to happen. In addition, Carl would be a big help in caring for the children during the long boat ride. ᘓ

Swedish ad for the Cunard line of steamboat travel. Johan and Selma may have read one like this.

Hej då (Good-bye)

October 18, 1904

A t the age of one year and four and a half months, Erik Knut Valdemar Sjöqvist clung to the neck of his mother, Selma. He was a toddler and could barely walk around the home of his mother and grandparents in Gränö.

Erik was a little fellow who seldom cried, but today was the exception to that rule. He sobbed as his Mormor pulled him from his Mor's neck. It was difficult to tell who was in more distress, mother or child.

Selma was leaving. She was taking Herman, John, and Ingeborg. It was with a heavy heart that she hugged Ester, the oldest child. She looked at her little eight-year-old daughter who was inconsolable with the thought of being left behind. Her tiny body shook with gigantic sobs.

Turning her eyes to her parents, Johan and Maria Dahlgren, Selma again viewed the quiet grief these two held within. Her father, Johan, bent down and picked up Ester in his strong arms. Her mother, Maria, held on tightly to baby Erik.

Selma felt like calling the whole thing off and abandoning this crazy idea of venturing off to North Dakota. How could she handle the misery she viewed in her loved ones?

Just then there was a knock at the door. Carl Johansson arrived to assist Selma with Herman, John, and Ingeborg. He was young and full of optimism and energy.

"Well, let's go! Come on boys. Herman and John you help your Mor. Take my hand little Ingeborg."

Selma gave quick farewells, but she gave a special squeeze to her little baby. "Whew! This is not easy!" She turned quickly and closed the door following Carl as the tears flowed unstopped down her cheeks.

Carl gently guided the little flock to the train station. They boarded the train for the ride to Göteborg in Västergötland, Sweden. They commenced the very first leg of a long, tiring, and unforgiving journey. ∞

Central Train Station in Göteborg, Sweden (2014). Johan, Selma, and eventually all their children would have arrived here on their way to America.

"God is our refuge and strength, an ever-present help in trouble. Therefore we will not fear, though the earth give way and mountains fall into the heart of the sea."

Psalm 46:1-2

We're Off!

October 1904

"Göteborg will be the beginning of our ocean voyage," Selma explained to the three youngsters. "We are almost there now. The first boat will take us from here to England and the second one all the way to America." Their train had just arrived at the outskirts of Göteborg on the western coast of Sweden.

Even before the train stopped, Selma gathered their personal belongings and made certain the children were ready to disembark. She then set-

Postgatan or Sillgatan (Herring) Street where tickets were purchased

tled back in her seat as the locomotive slowed its advancement into the city center of Göteborg. She would need to bolster her courage for the next step of their journey.

Stepping from the train, they noticed people were moving hither, thither, and yon. The area around the platform was dark, sooty, and full of combustion. Trains were moving forward with whistles blowing while others were stopping with the loud screech of metal wheels on the tracks. Everyone moved with haste and appeared to know exactly where they were headed.

Leaving the train station, Carl explained, "It's important we find Herring Street as quickly as possible. Soon, it will be dark and we need to buy our tickets before the offices close. The entire street is composed of steamship company offices. We're going to look for the office of J. Oscar Reis. This is the same place that Johan purchased his tickets for passage. Agents here will help us get our travel tickets."

The Cunard Line office and staff at 28 Postgatan in Göteborg, Sweden (1911). Johan and Selma bought tickets here.
Below: Postgatan Street (2014)

There was no mistaking the reason the street had such a strange name. "I think we must have arrived," Carl stated the obvious. The strong, pungent smell of rotten fish confronted them. This street was near the ocean and its famous fish market.

"Ja! We're here! That smell is ugly," Herman remarked. They all laughed at his wrinkled up nose.

It was on the smelly Postgatan Street, better known as Sillgatan (which means herring), that Carl Johansson purchased five tickets from a Cunard line agent J. Oscar Reis. He used the money Johan had sent with him. The tickets would take them all the way to Estevan in Canada. In Estevan they would buy additional railway passage to Kenmare, North Dakota. It would get them close to their final destination of Johan's homestead.

After an emotional and exhausting first day of travel, the little group found a rooming house. Their room was sparse with barren walls and narrow little beds. Before falling

asleep, Selma prayed for protection in the upcoming days.

    ❧ EARLY THE NEXT MORNING on a bright, sunny October 21st, Carl, Selma, and her children entered the large Emigration Building located near the docks. They were eager to get all tickets and paperwork processed here.

    Once this was accomplished, the two adults and trio of children stepped onto the docks. In front of them sat the big ship *Calypso*, which would take them across the North Sea to Hull, England.

    Selma stopped short. Suddenly, she realized that with the next few steps she would be leaving her dear homeland of Sweden. For a moment she questioned her decision, but the desire to be with Johan was like a mighty magnet pulling her forward. Taking her children by the hand they all took the steps needed and embarked. Once everyone with tickets was on deck, the *Calypso* pushed off from shore. Selma sadly watched as her homeland disappeared from sight. Deep inside she questioned when, if ever, she could or would return.

    The small group arrived in Hull, England and began the next leg of the journey. Here they boarded another train and traveled through the English countryside to Liverpool. Selma was tired and apprehensive of what lay ahead. Before she had time to close her eyes and rest, they were pulling into the Liverpool train station.

    Putting any questioning feelings aside, Selma joined Carl and the children, along with their luggage in a carriage provided by the steamship company. They were taken to boardinghouses for overnight lodging. The men were assigned to one boardinghouse, the women to another.

    Sleep was elusive for Selma as she tossed and turned on the smelly old bed in the cheap boardinghouse. Her greatest fears were in boarding the huge steamship in the not too distant future. On this large vessel they would spend two weeks cramped in tight quarters. Their destination across the un-

Rooming houses across from the Emigration Building where many emigrants stayed (2014)

predictable Atlantic Ocean would be Boston. In the wee hours of the early morning, Selma finally dropped off into a restless, fitful sleep.

On October 25, 1904, Carl, Selma, and her three youngsters took a giant step in their journey when they readied to board the huge vessel, *Saxonia*. After leaving the boarding house, Carl guided the little group to the Liverpool wharf. Selma looked at the gigantic ocean liner docked in front of them. She wondered how it could ever stay afloat. It was so large that her entire village with all its houses, barns, shops, and churches could easily fit into the ship. It was difficult to conceive this giant in front of her would be their home for the next several days.

People were everywhere! There were more people down on the docks than she had ever in her life seen together in one place; more than 2,000 other passengers crowding onto the pier with shabby clothes and tattered bundles and bags. Selma listened to the chattering of various languages.

Sixteen hundred had purchased passage in third class or steerage. This level of travel had few comforts, but offered the very cheapest passage.

The farther Selma traveled from Sweden and her home, the more impossible it seemed that she could ever return. They were about to cross a body of water so vast it would take 14 days to reach the other side. The Atlantic

Calypso boat that Selma took from Göteborg to Hull, England

Emigration Building, Göteborg, Sweden

Göteborg Harbor

Farewell to home; emigrants bound for England and America on a steamer at Göteborg, Sweden. *Photo: Underwood & Underwood (1905)*

Ocean lay before her. Her stomach ached at the very thought. She had never imagined a world so big and overwhelming as this one. And they weren't even to America yet.

Selma and Carl had their hands full trying to keep track of each other. They hung on tightly to the children's hands as they lugged their heavy totes and bundles. Boarding with the large mass of people pushing and shoving and calling out to loved ones added even more noise, frustration, and anxiety to an already difficult situation.

Once on board Carl spotted an open area close to the railings. Motioning for Selma and Ingeborg to follow him, he guided the boys to have a "front row seat" to their departure. The cool breeze hit Selma's face and the clouds overhead added to the melancholy feelings Selma had within her. She watched as the coastline slowly began to shrink into a far off distance. The span between the ship and Liverpool's port grew wider and wider. The dock became smaller and smaller as *Saxonia* chugged and picked up speed.

Selma felt Ingeborg squeeze her hand as the little girl held on tight to her Mor. Looking down into her face Selma saw fear of the unknown radiate from the face of her innocent child. Selma immediately knew that she needed to take charge and create a positive attitude. She could and would be brave and strong for her little ones.

"We are off on a wonderful adventure, but you cannot leave this spot without telling either Mr. Johansson or me." Selma looked into the children's eyes with loving firmness. "Just think Herman, John, and Ingeborg. Soon we will see Far. Won't that be great?"

℘ LEAVING THE RAILING, the small group searched for the third class steerage section, deep in the belly of the *Saxonia*. As they wove their way through throngs of people, Selma realized the high price this voyage was costing Johan. For the umpteenth time she felt her pocket to be certain the $20 she carried was still with her. This was a lot of money and she absolutely could not lose it. Any food or other needs along the way would need to be met from these funds.

Days passed and no matter where Selma went on the ship she couldn't get away from all the foul smells surrounding her. In steerage Selma's berth was eighteen inches wide, six feet long, and four feet high. She shared this with her daughter, Ingeborg. Herman and John shared another. It was dark with minimal lighting. Because there was no way for bathing and limited wa-

S. S. Saxonia

ter for washing, hordes of people reeked from perspiration. In addition many people were sick and the results added to the stench. Everyone was packed together like herring in a barrel. The smell was far worse than rotten fish!

Selma yearned to breathe the fresh ocean air. If the weather was good she would venture up on deck. But, instead of a clean cool mist, all she could breathe were stinky cigarettes smoked by dozens of men. Now, she realized how she had taken for granted the wonderful sweet air back home. She thought of the aroma of hay, pine trees, wet grass, flowers, and even the barnyard.

Their ship was heading for the port of Boston in America. Selma had added comfort knowing that Johan had been on this very same ship in March of 1903. Maybe she was sitting in the exact same spot he sat or walking on the very planks he had walked. Although it was only one and a half years later, it felt like an entire lifetime to her. She missed her husband so. ∽

Note: In the early 1900s steerage fares averaged about $25. This included passage from the United Kingdom to the United States of America. During mid-1904 through early 1905 a fare war existed. It was known as the 1904 Fare War and steerage passage went as low as $10 to $15. Some even offered family fare rates. This was well below the break even point for companies.

Göteborg harbor (2014)

"...but those who hope in the LORD will renew their strength. They will soar on wings like eagles; they will run and not grow weary, they will walk and not be faint."

Isaiah 40:31

She Must Walk!

November 2, 1904

The journey across the seas was long and rough. One day melted into another day as time drug on slowly. Ever so slowly. There was little to do on board. Even though Selma had sewing and knitting along, the constant movement of the ship made it all impossible.

Carefully each and every day, Selma portioned out the cheese, crackers, and fish that she had brought along. The food provided by the ship's officers had a foul smell and the soup was so thin it looked like a broth. By being careful they would have enough to make it all the way to Boston. She knew it wouldn't be enough to fill the stomachs of active youngsters. So, sometimes Selma scrimped on her own portions adding it instead to the children's.

Days passed as the little group bolstered each other's spirits. Carl had made this journey years before and knew what to anticipate. Just when Selma would lose hope or need assistance with one of the children, Carl would suddenly appear. "Hey, boys, if it's ok with your Mor, would you two young men like to go up on deck for a while?" He took them where they could see the giant waves. They were amazed that the water was so vast. They couldn't see the other side. "Where did the land go?" they asked Carl.

Carl would chuckle and explain the best he could to these two active, but bright young lads. "They will be a big help to Johan with all their energy," he thought.

During these times of quiet, Selma could relax a little more. Little Ingeborg would play quietly beside her. Sometimes, she'd even snuggle up

1904 Immigrant
Landing Station,
Boston

to her Mor, when her mother dozed off for a few moments. As time wore on, Selma began to worry that her daughter was finding it difficult to stand and walk. "Oh, she'll be alright. She just doesn't have her sea legs yet," Selma reassured herself.

What joy! On a quiet, clear day, November 2nd, Carl came to wake Selma. It was early, really early, and everything was very dark down in third-class. "What is the matter?" Selma whispered. She didn't want him rousing the children. "Why are you waking me up now? The children are still sleeping."

Carl was too excited to be quieted. "Land has been spotted off in the distance. Get your things together and we'll go up on deck to see it for ourselves. Hurry now, children."

Once on deck Selma *could* see for herself. It was just a slight hint of land off in the haze. She looked in the opposite direction from where the ship was headed. Off to the east, she could see the first streaks of dawn. It was then that the captain's voice was heard. "We will be landing at 7 a.m. Be sure to get your things ready. We will need information from you before you are allowed to leave the vessel."

America lay waiting for her. Selma was so eager to get to North Dakota and once again see Johan. Her heart raced double time with sweet anticipation. She was unaware of the long land journey that still lay ahead. Even if she had known, Selma wouldn't have cared. She just wanted to get her feet on solid ground once again.

There was one giant obstacle before any of this could happen. Everyone, including the children, was expected to walk the gang plank as they departed the ship. This would prove to the immigration authorities they were healthy enough to enter the new land. Failing to do so could result in detention and provide a possible reason for deportation. For some unknown medical reason, little Ingeborg was still finding it difficult to walk. Selma's mind whirled with all the possible scenarios of what could happen.

Once again her big Swedish/American friend came to the rescue. Selma and Carl devised a plan. They prayed it would work. Their little group would be the first in line and Carl would carry Ingeborg over his shoulder. Little three-year-old Ingeborg was to pretend she was sleeping. No matter what, she could not move!

One by one Selma and the other children walked down the gang plank. When it came time for Mr. Johansson and Ingeborg to begin, they were only a few steps on their walk, when the ship's officer shouted, "Put the child down! She must walk for herself."

Ingeborg knew she must keep pretending as her big friend replied, "Would you be so cruel as to require such a silly rule of a little sleeping child? Come on. Let us pass."

It took a few anxious moments, while the ship's officer surveyed the situation. People were lined up behind the man and little child. Everyone was eager to disembark. With disgust in his voice he replied, "Well okay then, be off with you two!"

Selma was so happy when they were all safe and sound on dry land. After walking around for some time little Ingeborg got her bearings and eventually was able to walk normally again.

Together the group entered the Immigrant Landing Station on the East Boston pier. Selma was surprised that the inspection process went so well. Ingeborg passed with flying colors.

Carl took charge as he guided Selma and the children from the landing station to the train station. She marveled at his mastery of the English language. He made it look so easy as they maneuvered through all the questions that needed to be answered.

Entering the railroad passenger car, Selma settled back in her chair. Every step brought her closer to the homestead. She and her children were heading for the promises of this rich, new land. America lay before them. And, Johan was waiting in North Dakota! ∞

"Be strong and courageous, and do the work. Do not be afraid or discouraged, for the Lord God, my God, is with you. He will not fail you or forsake you ..."

1 Chronicles 28:20

Arriving on the Homestead

1904 – 1905

The train ride half way across the United States and Canada was long and tedious for Selma and the children. Carl was again the lifesaver. He kept her and the youngsters listening with rapt attention as he told them of life in Dakota. "The coyotes howl at night and you can hear the ducks, geese, and birds all day long."

"The place where your Far has built a house for you is in the most beautiful spot ever. Your homestead lies in the foothills of the Mouse River. It has a most wonderful view. In the coulees there are berries just waiting to be picked. You'll find juneberries, chokecherries, plums, wild strawberries, and more."

Carl continued by looking straight at Herman and John. "And if you two go to the river, you'll probably be able to catch a passel of fish for supper. And when you get a little older, maybe you can even get a deer or two and end up with enough to last all winter."

Both Herman and John's faces were a display of eager attention, but when Selma looked at little Ingeborg she couldn't repress her laughter. Her daughter's eyes were huge from the first mention of coyotes howling.

At Estevan in Canada the group switched trains. As they headed south to Kenmare, North Dakota, Selma knew they were on the very last leg of their journey. Nothing would compare with the feeling of finally being able to be in the arms of Johan. It couldn't happen too soon for her.

As the train chugged down the tracks, the rhythm of the wheels matched the beat of Selma's heart. It seemed to say, "I'm coming, Johan. I'm coming, Johan."

Carl had forecast each and every stop along the way. He excitedly said, "Kenmare's next." Selma gathered her belongings and readied the children to disembark.

When at last the train began to slow down and the conductor officially announced that the train was pulling into the Kenmare depot, everyone was ready. The three children sat with their faces pressed against the windows. Who could spot Far first?

It seemed to take forever before the locomotive finally came to an abrupt stop in front of the train depot. John spotted his Far, "There he is! There's Far!!"

Selma let the children descend from the train car. Ingeborg flew into her father's arms. After twirling her around, Johan set her down on the train platform and surrounded an arm around each of his sons. Above their heads his eyes searched for Selma. Where was she?

At last Carl came into view carrying the luggage. Close behind him was

Rolling hills of the homestead leading down to the river valley

the vision he had searched, waited, and longed for all these months. Selma. His Selma! She was here at last!!

Upon seeing Selma, Johan rushed to her and held her tight. Holding her face in his rough, calloused hands he tenderly wiped the tears of joy that ran down her cheeks. "You're here! You're here!! Now I can do anything and everything. As long as I have you by my side."

ᔕ CARL HADN'T EXAGGERATED the beauty of the homestead. The pathway of the meandering river with its multiple trees opened to a valley of rolling hills that surrounded it. In many ways their new setting reminded Selma of Sverige, the homeland they had left behind.

Johan was delighted to have his wife, Selma, by his side. He had missed her in the year and seven months they had been apart. It had seemed like a lifetime of separation. Before her arrival he felt like the loneliness would engulf him with discouragement and fears.

As the young couple stood in front of the small, bare house they would call "home," Johan knew that it was far removed from any frills and extravagance. He had hoped to have more of the finishing work done on the interior before Selma arrived.

Johan's thoughts were interrupted when he heard Selma's voice.

"Oh, I love it! I really, really love it," Selma declared. Her sincerity shone in her eyes which brimmed with unshed tears. She simply marveled at all the work her husband had accomplished.

Johan looked at her lovingly. "I promise that things will be better in a few years. I'll work even harder to make it happen."

Selma pondered his words "in a few years." Was Johan planning to stay? She shrugged off the thought and cushioned her thinking. "Just until we accumulate our wealth," was her comfort.

But nothing, not one thing could replace the love this young couple shared and the dreams they held. The future which lay before them was especially evident as they watched their precious children. Johan never tired from watching his two young sons and little daughter as they worked and played together. He marveled at how much they had grown in his absence.

Johan thought back over the past months without his family. Each day he arose long before dawn to do the animal chores. Later in the morning Johan hooked up the oxen to break the sod. The hard, broken soil needed tilling and only after this was completed could it be followed by the planting of precious, golden kernels.

At the end of each day, Johan just couldn't believe how tired he was. Sometimes he could work feverishly into the night. He was frantic to complete more on the house. At other times, he was so exhausted he'd flop on the bed without washing up or having enough energy to eat supper. His house was a far cry from the regal homes found up and down the river. Other homesteaders had come many years before he had arrived. These farms were well established, and their homes were large and elegant. Johan could provide a place for his family to sleep and cook, and also a limited area for his children to play inside. But the best playground of all was the vastness of the wide open spaces right out their front door.

And so, as Johan watched over his family, he was so grateful for their safe arrival. Deep inside he yearned with profound longing to see his eldest daughter, Ester. And little Erik. A son he'd never seen. What did this son look like? Everyone spoke of his calm, quiet nature and his overall gentleness. Would this get in the way of the rough and tough trip across the giant waters when it was his turn to come to America? He hoped not.

After arriving in North Dakota Selma worked side by side with Johan as they labored intensively to established their new home. In reality, work

Mouse River

far outbalanced the play. There was no end to the monumental tasks that lay before them. There was ground to till and animals were needed for this undertaking. But each time an animal was purchased more labor was added. It took more time, energy, and money to acquire feed and hay. These new animals needed care and tending on a daily basis. All this, added to an already abundant workload.

When the tasks seemed daunting and impossible to accomplish, Selma and Johan put their faith and trust in God. Through Him they drew courage and support to continue the tireless, unending efforts before them. They had each other and three of their children with them in this New Land. They were so thankful.

While all this gave them comfort, Selma felt strong tugs to Sweden. Not only had she left her beloved homeland, but she had left her parents and two of her children behind. How long would it be before she'd lay eyes on her precious son and daughter? Each night she placed them safely in the hands of God, asking for an extra abundance of strength for her parents that cared for them. She knew her children were well loved, but active youngsters made lots of demands on her aging parents. In addition to prayers, Johan reassured her, "All will be well."

Johan knew when Selma longed for Sweden. She would step outside their home, look around, and he would hear her say, "This reminds me so much of Sverige. I feel like I'm back home again."

Selma viewed the large trees near the river. They offered an abundance of shade and the slow-moving river as it lapped on the banks was cool and refreshing. The tall wheat and grasses waved in the winds, bringing her thoughts closer to a faraway land that would always be dear.

As their faith grew, times continued to challenge Selma and Johan to their very core. Crops did not yield gold. And they were constantly struggling to make ends meet. Sometimes the North Dakota soil and rains produced an abundance of grains. Other times it was slim to none. They were young and their backs resilient to never-ending farm work. There was little else to do. They thanked God for good health and sound minds. Then, they persevered. ∞

A Growing Family

1905 – 1909

The one thing that continued to grow was their family. A daughter, Ruth Josephina Helena, arrived on August 10, 1905. When she entered the world, Johan looked at her and said, "Why you're just as cute as a button." Selma smiled. "She looks just like her big sister, Ingeborg."

What a delight it was on May 6, 1907 to have yet another new baby in the family. A son, Edwin Sigmund Herbert, gave Johan and Selma joy beyond measure. This little fellow reminded Selma of their son Erik. The couple felt so blessed. Now they had five children in America and two in

Sjöqvist family by their homestead claim shack: John, Johan & Ruth, Ingeborg, Selma & Edwin, and Herman (probably late 1907 or early 1908)

Sweden. This included four boys and three girls. Both Selma and Johan knew there were many challenges ahead of them to reunite their family.

Each child added to the young family brought more permanence to Johan and Selma staying in America. Instead of focusing on their return to Sweden they became more aware of their family needs. They desired more space to house their larger family. The original home was 12 feet wide and 26 feet long. Johan had built it with the help of 17-year-old Joseph Knudson. Aron Johnson had referred to his brother-in-law, Joseph, in his original letter to Johan and Joseph's help was most valuable. When the home was completed in late 1903, Aron assisted Johan's move into the dwelling on January 1, 1904.

Once Selma came with the three children it didn't take very long for the young couple to realize that more living space was an absolute necessity. With the two new American babies added to the family, Johan knew adding onto the home needed to be top priority in his ever-growing list of needs.

In late 1908, Johan removed the small entryway that had been attached to the end of the house and replaced it with an addition. Their new L-shaped dwelling added much-needed living and sleeping quarters on two levels. Selma and Johan were pleased and satisfied.

Selma smiled at her husband, "I could be happy living anywhere with you, Johan. But, having more room to live and work is a luxury I have always dreamed of and had great desire for. Thank you, Johan. *Tack*!" ☙

Sjöqvist family outside their home: John, Johan & Ruth, Ingeborg, Selma & Edwin, and Herman (1909)

"Do not forsake your friend and the friend of your father, and do not go to your brother's house when disaster strikes you - better a neighbor nearby than a brother far away."

Proverbs 27:10

Neighbors

1903 – 1915

Aron Johnson *(left)*

Reuben, Nora, Ellen, Aron Johnson *(below)*

What a blessing to be surrounded by other Scandinavian families. They understood the same language, enjoyed the same holidays, endured the same hardships, and cried over similar losses. Johan and Selma knew that homesteading would have been next to impossible without the invaluable help of the Johnson/Jonson brothers.

According to the Homestead Act of 1862, Johan was not allowed to leave the homestead for any length of time. Therefore, Johan was prohibited from traveling to Sweden to assist Selma in her big venture to America. Carl had come to his rescue! Carl had lost interest in his homestead when farming replaced free range cattle ranching. Carl wanted out. He had plans of selling his land to another farmer, Mons Brekhus. But if he owned land and property, getting in and out of the United States would be a lot easier. He was also a naturalized citizen, but he was eager to return to Sweden for a visit. For all of these reasons Carl volunteered to help his friend

Johan. Within three and a half months after his return with Selma and the children Carl Johan Jonson had completed his land transaction. He sold his 160-acre homestead on February 24, 1905 for $2,400. He left the area and never returned.

Joseph (Joe) Knudson

When Selma and children arrived, she and Johan continued to rely heavily on their other neighbors. This young couple borrowed farming equipment such as plows and oxen from Aron Johnson. Equipment and animals were shuffled back and forth according to where they were needed. Neighbors also assisted Selma and Johan in learning homesteading and naturalization expectations.

Farther down the river to the southwest lived Aron Johnson's brother-in-law and Nora's brother. Joseph Knudson was a Norwegian who came to the valley from Minnesota back in 1901. Johan met 17-year-old Joseph when he arrived in Grover Township and later worked with him in building the house on Johan's homestead. Both Johan and Selma often commented to each other. "It is a good thing that these neighbors are here. I doubt that we'd make it without them."

Ole Syverson

Ole Syverson lived to the north. The Mouse River meandered through his homestead. Ole was a quiet man and a great thinker. His deep faith was especially profound to all those in the valley. He offered many ideas of how to succeed even when things looked dismal. He was a man of few words, amazing wisdom, and a kind heart.

For years Ole had the best garden around. He freely shared garden produce and his strawberries were enjoyed by many. All Ole asked was for help in the picking and harvesting of his God-given bounty.

Another blessing to the area was the Swedish family of N. P. (Nils Peter) Swenson and his wife Martha who came to Dakota in 1872. They lived close to the settlement of McKinney. Although Johan seldom asked for their help, they had been sponsors for many other new immigrants coming into the area, giving generous support. The Swensons were proof that this new land could bring success. They were settled and able to extend their labors into assisting the area's growth. They were involved in building churches and schools, as well as, the community of McKinney.

The Swenson home, the finest in the area, was rebuilt in 1903. It was huge for these early homesteading years in America. The house measured 34 by 36 feet and was two stories high, using 18-foot long posts. Electric lights were installed and a well under the house pumped water into the kitchen above.

The Swensons were humble, helpful, and honorable people. Their success gave renewed energy to Selma and Johan as they planned, scrimped, and saved for their own homestead.

Mr. & Mrs. N. P. Swenson

Swenson Farm House (1903-1907)

John and Marie Servold lived on a homestead two and a quarter miles north of Johan and Selma. They were immigrants from Norway and came by train to Kenmare, North Dakota in 1904.

On their farm in Grover Township John and Marie raised five children. Lawrence, Carl, and Johanna never married and lived their entire life on their parents' farm. Annie married and lived in California. Emma also married and lived in Flaxton, North Dakota.

Their home was situated at the top of the hills overlooking the Mouse River. Deep coulees were in their backyard. The family had a black and white dog that would chase down the ravines after a tire. Dog lovers would roll a black, car tire from the top and watch the dog run. Finding it at the bottom the animal would put his body through the center of the tire and drag it up to the top.

Johanna Servold and Ruth Sjöqvist followed the harvest crews while working in the cook cars. They developed a strong friendship. This friendship continued throughout their lives, even when thousands of miles separated them. ∽

Johanna's mother Marie Servold, Ruth, Johanna Servold, and Selma (1954)

*"Day after day they pour forth speech;
night after night they display knowledge.
There is no speech or language where
their voice is not heard."*

Psalm 19:1-2

English, Please

1904 – 1915

The one-room Grover School the children attended was west of the river and the Sjöqvist children loved to cross the mighty Mouse River on their ice skates in the wintertime. It shortened their route so they could arrive at their destination more quickly. When it was sunny and warm everyone walked the longer way to school. Regardless, the weather seldom stopped them from attending.

Swedish was spoken by the Sjöqvist children at home. On the playground they shared their common language, but everyone was encouraged to use English in the confines of the school building. Lessons were taught in the language of this new land.

One winter day as the Sjöqvist children bounded through the door after school, Selma listened to them. Her children continued to laugh, giggle, and communicate in Swedish. How could she ever come to learn this new English language? Right then and there, she made a decision. She needed her children's help.

Grover School near the Joseph Knudson farm

"From now on, I want all of you to talk English when you come home. I must learn this new language and you need to help me. I so seldom go anywhere to hear English. I must learn English if I am to live in this new country. I need you to teach me."

In time Selma came to learn the language of her new land. It took many reminders for the children to assist her. They loved their native tongue and slipped easily in and out of English to Swedish and back to English again. Each time the children reverted back to Swedish Selma gently reminded them of their promise to help her.

There was one place though where only Swedish was acceptable. Selma wrote in her native tongue the multiple letters that were sent across the ocean to her children and parents. Ester and Erik and her parents replied in Swedish. When a response would come, it was a time of great rejoicing. Each letter was read and reread many times. Selma's heart ached with a great longing. She wanted to hold these children close to her once more. Doubts constantly nagged her. "Would it ever happen?"

"If and venn my kids do come, denn I vill teach dem Ink-lish all by myself. Ja, ya bet!!" ∞

Students at the Grover School (Spring or Fall of 1914): Wilbur Schweitzer, Augusta Swenson, Edwin Sjöqvist (front), Esther Swenson, Swen Swenson, Gordon Swenson, Mae Swenson, Cyril Axtell, Winifred Fitch (teacher), Ruth Sjöqvist (front), Eddie Rowland, Hazel Axtell, Gertrude Schweitzer, Lillian Syverson, Nels Olson, Bertha Olson, Ingeborg Sjöqvist (back), Carl Syverson, Ellen Johnson, Ruben Johnson

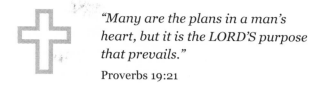

"Many are the plans in a man's heart, but it is the LORD'S purpose that prevails."

Proverbs 19:21

Documents

1903 – 1909

North Dakota offered challenges unique to itself. It was either too hot or too cold, too wet or too dry. Seldom were things calm and consistent. Through these obstacles Selma and Johan continued to work hard and count their blessings.

They would eventually own their property. They had a large-enough piece to eke out a living; 160 acres, an amount unheard of in Sweden. Johan never doubted that things would improve and get even better. He shared this belief with his devoted wife, Selma. Together they forged ahead with deep convictions and plans for a wonderful life in America.

The Homestead Act stated all settlers must file two applications for naturalization. This was a requirement for free land. Johan's neighbors encouraged him to do this immediately. And so, Johan first applied for citizenship on July 6, 1903. The papers were signed by John Lynch, the Clerk of District Court in and for Ward County, North Dakota.

Once Johan's citizenship was applied for, he could file on his homestead in Grover Township. So, two days later on July 8, 1903, Johan paid $14 for fees collected by the register and receiver, F. E. Fox, in Minot, North Dakota.

After five years had passed, Selma realized that Johan wanted to remain in this new country forever. The original dream of returning to Sweden after gaining great wealth was long past reality. In her mind Selma came to grips with the fact that she would never go back to Sweden. She would never see her parents again. Her new dream was to have her two children in Sweden join the family in America.

The year 1908 was important for Johan and Selma. On June 19, Johan completed the second petition for naturalization. Two of his neighbor friends were witnesses for him: Aron A. Johnson and Joseph Knudson from Tolley, North Dakota verified that Johan Sjöqvist was a United States resident. Now all they could do was wait for the legal wheels to turn. They knew it would take at least six weeks because one of the requirements was to publish that Johan A. Sjöqvist was proving his homestead claim. The *Mouse River Journal* newspaper published this notice for six consecutive weeks, beginning August 21, 1908. If anyone had a problem with the final homestead claim of Johan A. Sjöqvist they were to step forward and make a case against him.

(Not Coal Land.)
Serial No. 01083
Department Of The Interior.
Land office at Minot, N. D... Aug. 10, 1908.
Notice is hereby that John A. Sjoquist, of Barber, N. D., who on July 8, 1903, made H. E. Serial No. 01083. No. 23842, for W½ NE¼, E½ NW¼, Section 28, Township 162 N. Range 86W, Fifth P. Meridian, has filed notice of intention to make final five year proof, to establish claim to the land above described, before J. E. Smith, Clerk of District Court, Ward county, N. D., at Minot, N. D., on the 2nd day of October, 1908.
Claimant names as witnesses:
Aaron Johnson, Joseph Kudson, of Tolley, N. D. Nels W. Knudsen, Andrew Olson, of McKinney, N. D.
fp 8-21
L. D. McGahan, Register.

An unanticipated holdup dealt with Joseph Knudson's affidavit verifying Johan. Joseph's last name had been misspelled in the paperwork. It was held for additional written testimony. Joseph had to verify that Joseph Kudson was one and the same as Joseph Knudson.

After three and a half months, on an early fall day Johan returned with the mail. He had gone up the river to the Barber bridge where a grocery store with a post office received all local mail. The gentleman handed him an official-looking envelope. "This looks important. You'd better handle it carefully so it doesn't bend or tear."

Johan entered his home and gathered everyone together. "We've got some important mail. Come and see. Let's open it together. Here, Selma, you do the honors."

Selma received the large envelope and carefully opened it. "Oh, Johan! Our papers have arrived. Children this is really a special day. Listen and Far will read what it says."

Johan held the official document. "Let me read it and then you can all look at it. It is dated October 2, 1908 and this is our family naturalization paper. Myself, Mor, and all seven of you have been naturalized. This even includes your brother and sister in Sweden. Look down here. It was signed by J. E. Smith, Clerk of District Court, of Ward County, North Dakota. Do you know what this means?"

Johan and Selma waited for a reaction as they looked into the eyes of their five children.

"Are we legal now?" asked seven-year-old Ingeborg.

"Well, yes. This means we are now legally U.S. citizens. This is a really, really big day!" Far replied. And with a hoot and a holler from most every kid, the family sat down to supper.

A few days later another official paper arrived. This one was dated October 5 of the same year, 1908. Johan had paid $5.25 for his homestead paperwork. The final paper of land ownership was secured on May 27, 1909. Their homestead in Grover township was now legally owned by Johan and Selma Sjöqvist.

It was another opportunity for "hooting-and-hollering"!

℘ FOR OVER FIVE YEARS from the time of Johan's arrival and later Selma's coming, this hard-working family tilled the soil side by side. In 1903 Johan tilled six acres, in 1904 ten more acres, 1905 fifteen acres, 1906 twenty-nine acres for a grand total of sixty acres that were broken and cropped.

In addition to all the work of the soil, Johan built a 12- by 26-foot frame, shingled roof house and a 16- by 24-foot sod barn to house all the animals. A well had been dug and everything was fenced. All this required long, hard hours of backbreaking labor.

Even though the work was difficult, Johan had come to love his new home and the opportunities it offered his family. He was strongly motivated to provide for his wife and children. He rarely minded trading the sweat of his brow and the strength of his back to achieve peace and joy in knowing he had done so. He never doubted that he had made the right decision in coming to America. Together Selma and Johan thanked God for the bounties of the soil, whether large or small.

The children thrived. They attended school in the cold winters. In summer the river offered them cool and refreshing breaks. They swam in it and caught an abundance of fish for the family meals. In the deep ravines and coulees of their backyard they picked chokecherries, wild plums, and juneberries.

Life was good. ∞

Naturalization paper

Note: In the late 1800s and early 1900s Renville County had no organized county seat and all official paperwork, documents, etc. were issued by Ward County in Minot, North Dakota.

All legal papers stated Johan's name as John.

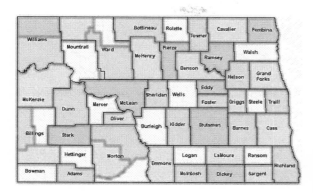

North Dakota Counties

Above: North Dakota counties in 1910 (current counties are shaded in the background.)

Right: County boundaries today.

Note: Ward County was reconfigured to create Renville County, Burke County and a smaller Ward County.

The Homestead Act of 1862

President Abraham Lincoln signed the Homestead Act and opened up the settlement of the Dakota Territory. The original Act was passed by Congress May 20, 1862 and took effect January 1, 1863. (The same day as the Emancipation Proclamation took effect.) By 1896 the land in North Dakota had been surveyed and opened for homesteading.

Eligibility: a person must be at least 21 years old, or the head of a family, or have met certain military requirements; must be a US citizen or have filed a declaration of intent; must not have taken up arms against the US government or given aid to the enemy (restriction was added as a result of the Civil War).

The eligible person would file an application with the register of the Land Office. An affidavit was taken stating the applicant had met the requirements and paid a $10 fee, as well as, a $2 commission to the land agent. The maximum amount of land was 160 acres or one quarter section in one contiguous piece of land.

A patent was an official document issued by the US Federal Government. It was the process of transferring Federal land to a homesteader after fulfilling the requirements. It was issued only once on a piece of land and would be signed by the President of the United States. (Any transfer of ownership after the original patent was done through a deed.)

The homesteader would obtain a patent certificate after: continuously residing on the land for 5 years; cultivating the land and making improvements.

When all requirements were met, the homesteader located two neighbors willing to vouch for the truth of his or her statements about the land's improvements and sign the "proof" document. After completing the final form and payment of a $6 fee, the homesteader received the patent for the land, signed by the President of the United States. The land now belonged to the homesteader.

The process could be shortened after six months of living on the land. The land could be purchased for $1.25 per acre.

North Dakota total acreage: 44,156,160 acres

Homestead acreage: 17,417,466 acres

Total percentage: 39%

Number of homesteads: 118,472

Land Terms

Abstract of Title - a summary of ownerships on a piece of land that has a title. The abstract is compiled by a private company using records from the county courthouse. It includes deeds, mortgages, leases, and other legal land events.

Deed - a written document when ownership of the land is transferred through a sale or gift.

Warranty Deed - when a land owner has a clear title and has the right to sell the land.

Quit Claim Deed - a document used when the land owner gives up all rights to the land.

Grantor - the person or entity transferring property.

Grantee - the person or entity acquiring property.

Contract for Deed - when a contract of agreement is made between the seller and buyer of property. The seller provides the financing and the buyer repays the loan in installments.

Mortgage - a lien put against property when securing a loan which is voided upon payments made according to agreed-upon terms.

Lien - a form of security interest by a governmental entity over property to secure the payment of a debt or other obligation.

Lease - a contract conveying land property, equipment, or facilities for a specified term and amount of rent.

Mineral Acres - minerals, gas, or petroleum beneath the surface of the land can be sold or leased to allow exploration and development of minerals. In 1930 the State of North Dakota allowed the surface acres and the mineral acres to be separated legally.

Plat - a drawing of an area depicting land ownership, blocks, lots, easements, roads, etc.

Township - 23,040 acres, with divisions of US Public Lands of 36 sections or square miles of land (6 miles x 6 miles).

Acre - 43,560 square feet or 4,840 square yards.

Section - 640 acres or one square mile.

Quarter - 160 acres (the amount of land a homesteader could obtain under the Homestead Act in North Dakota).

Lots - when originally surveying the land, there was an allowance for the curvature of the earth, lakes, and rivers; approximately 40 acres.

Survey - measurements made to determine the relative position of points on the earth's surface.

STRUGGLES

"My God, my God, why have you forsaken me? Why are you so far from saving me, so far from the words of my groaning? O my God, I cry out by day, but you do not answer, by night, and I am not silent."

Psalms 22:1-2

The Unthinkable

1910 - 1911

Everything changed one late spring day in 1910. Johan became ill. His headaches and sore throat were severe. At first he rested in the middle of the day. He could still complete the outside barn chores in the morning and evening. After a few weeks of little if any improvement, Johan went to see the doctor. On May 27th, Dr. Rainville examined Johan and advised him to take it easy.

Six weeks passed and Johan still felt so much pain. He had a constant fever and had lost considerable weight. Nothing seemed to give him relief. He decided to return to the doctor. This time he received some different advice and new ideas. Johan returned home.

As time dragged on, Johan found even the simplest outside tasks too difficult for his physical condition. He stayed in bed while the children went outdoors to feed and water the animals. They milked the cows and brought in the eggs. In the spring of 1911 the children followed their father's directions in tilling the fields and planting the crops.

Card of thanks in the Tolley newspaper, July 28, 1911

CARD OF THANKS.
We wish to express our sincere thanks to all our friends who so liberally subscribed to the Sjoquist Hospital Fund. May God bless you all.
—J. A. Sjoquist and family.

In July, Johan was hospitalized for a period of time. He had lost so much weight. His eyes were dull and his skin had an overall grayish tone.

That fall instead of attending school, Herman, John, and Ingeborg labored in the fields. And so, this 14-, 13-, and 10-year-old harvested the crops. They missed their school, their friends, and most of all, their father's guiding hands. Because Far spent most of his time in bed, many times the children had to figure out things the best they could with their youthful knowledge.

While Johan laid in bed, he requested Selma to come over close to him. She bent down. In a raspy, raw voice Johan pleaded with her. "I love you with all of my heart, but I would hate to believe that you get your strength only in me. God is the one who will always be there for you. You can't expect me to do His job. He is your stronghold."

At two a.m. on a cool fall night on October 3, 1911, Johan Alfred Sjöqvist left this life. He was still a young man at the age of 42 years, 5 months, and 29 days. Selma was a widow at the age of 41. She was left with five children in her home and two in Sweden. But, Johan had also left her with a dream. "America holds wondrous opportunities for the entire family."

Johan's body was kept at home until the day of the funeral, as was often the custom of the day. It was believed the deceased should have a loved one sit nearby day and night. The three older children and Selma took turns sitting beside their father and husband. Ten-year-old Ingeborg found it difficult to stay awake in the middle of the night. At last she thought of something that would keep her moving and alert. She took her father's comb and proceeded to style his hair one way and then another. She meant no disrespect. It was something she'd enjoyed doing while he was alive and she knew he'd always liked it.

Tolley Hospital
(Catholic church in
the background)

Selma's faith was being tested beyond limits. She remained strong in front of her children, but inside Selma struggled. Her heart ached with the loss of the one she loved. "Life hasn't turned out the way I'd like it to, but I just can't quit trying. Death makes life hard. Death is really the easy part—it's life that's hard."

Selma remembered Johan's words, "Rely on God." After sleepless nights and as anguish threatened to consume her, she gave up the turmoil and reached out to God. She leaned on God through her prayers. Slowly, she began to feel peace and calmness. She reassured her children, "All will be well." Inside, she dug deep to survive and to hold onto her husband's dreams for herself and their children. ❧

OBITUARY

In Memoriam of
Mr. John Sjoquist.

Died, at his home eight miles northeast of Tolley, on Monday of this week, John A. Sjoquist age 42 years. None but those who have set in the shadow of a great bereavement can justly weigh such a sorrow as the widow and children of this family have to bear. Those who have gone down in the valley of suffering and stood for months by the side of a loved one, as hope after hope dropped away as the petals fall from a fading flower, know that such anguish cannot find solace in the tenderest words.

Besides a devoted wife he leaves seven children two of which are in Sweden. We can only remind these mourners that he is not dead, he is only asleeping after a short and well spent life here.

The funeral services will be held today and the interment will be made in the McKinney cemetery.

The obituary for Johan A. Sjöqvist appeared in *The Tolley Journal* on October 6, 1911.

"Where you die I will die, and there I will be buried. May the Lord deal with me, be it ever so severely, if anything but death separates you and me."

Ruth 1:17

The Cold Earth

October 8, 1911

Selma continued to stand tall until she heard the hard, cold, black earth fall with a thud on the wooden coffin. This same black, North Dakota soil that was supposed to bring wealth and happiness now fell dreadfully heavy.

Thud.

Thud.

Thud.

It made an even pattern that matched Selma's heartbeats. Tears silently rolled down her face. There was no holding them back.

Her heart was breaking. Selma had just walked behind the casket at the Swedish Lutheran Church in Tolley. On the outside she held up well with limited tears. She worked hard to be a pillar of strength for her youngsters. But no one would ever really know the huge ache and gigantic hole she felt inside. Her partner, her husband, her helpmate, her lover, her other half had been ripped away from her.

As Selma walked with her children, she was numb to everything and everyone around her. Only the questions of her own children could jar her from the deep crevice she had fallen into. Her feelings were raw and excruciatingly painful.

The pastor said comforting words and the congregation prayed and sang songs in Swedish. All her friends and neighbors were in attendance. But to Selma, it was all a blur.

She knew it was necessary to contact loved ones in Sweden. Both Ester and Erik needed to know the loss of their Far. She would write to her children, parents, and to Johan's family. Out of his large family of parents and six children only one sister, Alma, remained. There was no hurry. Letters seemed to take forever to get across the vast Atlantic Ocean. But she would write.

And now she stood in the McKinney Cemetery for the burial. Early pioneers had been randomly buried in this same location. The cemetery was not officially organized, but her neighbors had helped in securing a plot for Johan to lay.

Evangelical (Swedish) Lutheran Church in Tolley, North Dakota (2012)

She snapped back to the demands of the living when one of the children tugged on her hand. Looking down, she gave eye contact and a half-hearted smile. "Let's go children. We need to get out of the way of these men as they finish their work."

Turning to leave, Selma saw that her two oldest sons had not responded. Both Herman and John continued to stare at the deep, dark hole that was slowly being filled in. Her heart broke for them and all of her children.

"Come boys. I need your help. Let's go."

Once all the youngsters were moving in the right direction, Selma stopped momentarily to look back at the place that held her dearly beloved Johan. "Your life may be over, but our love will forever grow in the hearts and lives of our children. Good-bye. I love you! *Min älskade* Johan (My beloved Johan)," she whispered. ∞

Note: As the years passed and the cemetery was organized, it was determined that Johan's gravesite was in the roadway or path between the many plots. The grave was never moved, but the tombstone was. It was placed in the Sjöqvist/Atwood section of the cemetery.

Scribed on the stone are the following words:

JOHAN ALFRED
SJÖQVIST

Född d.
(born the day of)
4 Apr. 1869.

Död d.
(died the day of)
3 Okt. 1911.

Saliga äro de
döda som i
Herranam dö.

(Blessed are the dead who die in the name of the Lord. Rev. 14:13)

"Keep falsehood and lies far from me;
give me neither poverty nor riches,
but give me only my daily bread."
Proverbs 30:8

An Empty Flour Bin

1912

Times were desperate for the Sjöqvist family. They had no money. In 1912 there was no federal aid or food stamps to assist families in need. Selma had five children in her home between the ages of four to fourteen. In addition, she had a fifteen-year-old daughter and an eight-year-old son in Sweden. Things could not look more dismal for the family.

The old statement, "when the going gets tough, the tough get going," could definitely apply to this family's situation. Herman, John, and Ingeborg entered the working world in order to bring money home to support their mother, brother, and sister.

Herman and John quickly found work on neighboring farms. Young men could be hired cheaply for hard, backbreaking labor. This was especially true during the long, fall harvest and then again in the spring. There was little time for fun and frolic. However, both of these young scrapping lads had strong desires to participate in all the extra curricular activities in life. Temptations lurked for them at every corner.

Ingeborg was a quick worker and once the word got out that she was seeking employment people sought her out. Sleeping in an upstairs bedroom with many hired hands in adjoining rooms was frightening. In order to feel more secure, she slept with all her clothes on and furniture piled in front of the bedroom door.

For a girl, Ingeborg was tall. She had gained her adult height by the age of ten. Keeping her age a secret, it was easy for her to be hired whenever a farm woman gave birth. Assistance was needed to tend to the other children, cook for the hired men, bake, clean house, garden, and more.

One day Ingeborg left home at the crack of dawn and walked four and a half miles to help a farm lady in need. After working all day she was elated to walk the four and a half miles home. It was dusk and she swung a pail of lard and 25 cents jingled in her pocket. The lard would be spread on bread in place of butter and the money would go to Selma, her Mor.

Selma stayed at home and cared for the younger children. Even when there was little if any flour in the bin, the children would hear her say, "God will provide." Her calm faith gave the three older children the drive and incentive to work and work harder.

Each and every Friday the three children were told to bring their earnings home to add to the family income. Even though the amount each of them earned was extremely limited, when added together they could make it. Barely.

℀ ONE FRIDAY EVENING, Ingeborg's two older brothers failed to arrive home for supper. The family waited and waited and still the two boys didn't come.

"I wonder what has happened to Herman and John?" Selma remarked each time she looked out the front door.

At last Ingeborg could take the frustration of her delinquent brothers no longer. "I'll be back," she called over her shoulder as she left the house.

Buckboards and buggies pulled by teams of horses were used prior to automobiles.

Taking the horses and buckboard, she headed to the road along the river. She had a sneaking suspicion where the boys were and what they were up to.

Using the buggy whip, she spurred the horses into a fast, steady gait. The farther she drove the more upset she became. Why couldn't these two be more reliable? Didn't they realize that their mother needed them and the money they earned?

Arriving at the home of the Swenson bachelor brothers, 11-year-old Ingeborg strode up to the front door. Her determination and demeanor were easily discernable by the look on her face. She was positive her brothers were inside.

Bursting through the kitchen door without knocking, Ingeborg entered, buggy whip in hand. She looked at the table inside the room. There sat both Herman and John. It was evident what was going on. Ingeborg was furious with what she saw in front of her. They were gambling away their hard earned money. Foolishly they were squandering it with these older men. In addition to the cards in their hands, they had colored liquid in glasses in front of them.

Ingeborg grabbed the bottles and glasses on the kitchen table. Taking quick steps to the sink, she proceeded to dump the liquor. Within seconds she was back to the small table. Holding her apron out in front of her, she scooped up the money on the table top.

She was angry. Her two big brothers knew it instantly. They grabbed their caps and headed for the door.

All that Ingeborg could utter under her breath was to say, "How could you? How could you do that to our Mor?"

Herman and John jumped in the back of the buckboard as Ingeborg flew out of the house and jumped up on the front seat. They heard the crack of the whip as the horses sped from the yard.

Dropping the two vagrants off at the front door at home, Ingeborg drove the buckboard and horses to the barn. She needed time alone.

Before going into the house she prayed that God would forgive her anger. "And while you're at it, God, why don't you straighten up those two brothers of mine. Without their help we'll never get Ester and Erik to America."

That night before she closed her eyes in sleep, Ingeborg made a vow to God. "I will never, ever let gambling, liquor, or other vices control me. You'll have to help me Lord because I never want them to be a part of my life."

Stopping, she added, "God help us all!" ∽

"Trust in the LORD with all thine heart; and lean not unto thine own understanding."

Proverbs 3:5

Nickels and Dimes

1912

Times were extremely difficult for Selma. While trying to make ends meet for food, clothing, and necessities in life, the family also desperately worked to put aside a few pennies for the two children's journey from Sweden.

Selma yearned with a great longing to see once more her son and daughter, Erik and Ester. At times it appeared to be a far off dream. Her children in America had needs of their own. They were growing up fast. The boys especially missed and needed the strong structure and guidance of their father. The big world offered adult temptations that were far beyond their years. At least Selma's children in Sweden had the influence of both her mother and father. This thought became her comfort and consolation.

Herman, her oldest son, loved to fix things. He could fix anything that broke or just refused to run. He was tall in stature like his father, Johan. He was softer spoken of the two older boys, but was the one easily misled by others. Selma prayed that the men he followed would be upright and of good character.

Her next oldest, John, was a lover of music. He also became good at repairing broken items. These were things usually damaged in his own hasty anger.

Somehow, through his work, John had acquired a violin. He delved into playing his new instrument with a feverous desire for perfection. His innate talent was often overshadowed by his quick temper. If things didn't sound right after a number of attempts, he would take and crack his violin over any close, hard object. It would break into a gazillion pieces. As a result, John spent hours repairing his beloved violin.

Once John was sitting on the banks of the meandering Mouse River. He was enjoying his violin and was working on a melody that he had heard recently. Time after time, he started over. When he'd get to the same spot in the song, he'd stop playing. It just didn't sound right.

Finally, in desperation he flung the violin. His strong arm made it sail through the air. Kerplop!! It landed in the middle of the river. In disbelief, John watched his treasured violin sink to the bottom of the mighty Mouse.

For days thereafter, he would go to the river. John was a wonderful swimmer. Dive after dive he went to the bottom of the Mouse. At last he retrieved his soggy violin from the murky mud. Needless to say, it took countless more hours to bring the water-soaked violin back to working order.

Selma's oldest daughter in America, Ingeborg, was very tall for her age and by ten years old she had gained all her height, appearing to be an adult. As a result, grownup expectations were too often placed on her young shoulders. Ingeborg accepted these responsibilities and became even stronger from them. She was a determined young lady with a soft heart for others, especially her family. She would work from sunup to sundown with nary a complaint.

Ingeborg loved the outdoors. She could handle the animals almost better than her big brothers. She especially enjoyed the family horses. Neighbors often remarked on her riding horsemanship. She gained quite a reputation for riding two horses together until they were at a full gallop. Rising above the two racing animals, she would stand with one foot on the back of each horse. Ingeborg had perfect balance and made a scene for any viewer passing by. Stunts like this became her release from hard, back-breaking labor.

Selma's youngest daughter, Ruth, stayed close to her. She helped around the house. She was so eager to please her Mor. She was somewhat softer than her older three American siblings, but she had also learned to hold her ground with them. She seldom felt the pressing need for income and the driving force behind the work ethics of Herman, John, and Ingeborg. After all, she was the baby girl of the family.

Edwin was the youngest. He was kind and gentle. He loved everyone and in return, he truly believed everyone loved him. They did. Edwin was easily hurt and somewhat fragile. The whole family looked out for him. They defended him from the barbs of those less kind.

And so, Selma and her five children in America struggled on a day-to-day basis. Beyond the hardships, they loved, laughed, and thanked God for the smallest of blessings.

The nickels and dimes saved for Sweden would accumulate and then quickly disappear. Some unpredictable need would occur and the entire fund would be wiped out. Time after time this happened. The farm had accumulated insurmountable and growing debts.

Trying to keep the farm operating while the three oldest worked outside the home and attended school for a few months in the winter became almost too difficult. This family had fierce determination, but the odds were against them.

At last, Selma had to make a decision. Would she hang onto their beloved farm and never again see her children in Sverige or should she part with the homestead that Johan had worked so hard for and try to locate something more manageable? This was the most difficult of decisions and one that she pleaded before the throne of God on a daily basis. What should she do? ∽

1912 Liberty head nickel

1912 Barber dime

"If there is a poor man among your brothers in any of the towns of the land that the Lord your God is giving you, do not be hardhearted or tightfisted toward your poor brother. Rather be openhanded and freely lend him whatever he needs."

Deuteronomy 15:7-8

In a World of Men

1912

One year after Johan's death, Selma knew she needed help. She was desperate for money. Her three oldest American children were off working, their earnings never bringing in enough to make ends meet. Herman was now 15, John was 13, and Ingeborg was 11. Selma had come to depend on them over the past year.

Many times Selma would go to her kitchen and see the bottom of the flour bin. A sure sign that times were tough. But, as long as she had some flour in the bin, she could bake bread. This meant there would always be *something* to eat. The children could hear her murmurings as she attempted to comfort herself. "The Lord will provide," she declared over and over again.

So, on the fifteenth day of October 1912, Selma relented and knew she had no other recourse. Her family desperately needed money to stay afloat. After a lot of thought she ventured off to the First National Bank of Kenmare, North Dakota.

Selma needed to secure a loan. While living with her husband, the two had never borrowed money from a lending establishment. This was a world foreign to her. Men ruled in the arena of business and finance. Women were seldom a part of it. Society merely frowned upon the weaker feminine sex coming to grips with such masculine roles.

But Selma's world had tipped upside down with her husband's passing. Although she had worked side by side with Johan, he had always been the leader of the two. He had been good at making sound decisions in regards to his loved ones.

In 1912 a woman usually gained her identity from the husband she married. Selma had always been known as Mrs. Johan Sjöqvist, not Selma Sjöqvist. With Johan's death, Selma found herself doing things that previously she had felt were impossible. Going to a bank was one of them. She had to bolster herself to do this daunting task. The hunger of her children gave her the courage.

First National Bank (far right) of Kenmare, ND, prior to 1917

As she entered the bank, she noted it was filled with men. She was definitely out of her league. But, she refused to be intimidated by the situation. Selma squared her shoulders and got in line.

When it came to her turn, the banker appeared to ignore her. Instead, he looked around her and beckoned the next man in line to step forward.

"Excuse me sir, but I do believe I am next," she said in her broken English. She was determined not to be pushed around by this tiny man behind the counter.

"Yes. Is that your husband behind you?" the banker asked.

"No. I really don't know dat man."

The banker looked confused and even more frustrated. "Well, what do you want then?"

"I need some money." She answered quickly, before she lost the little confidence within her. If she hadn't been so desperate, Selma might have turned and marched right out.

"That's a story I've heard many times today. What else is new?" the man snidely remarked.

Selma stood her ground. "Can I get a loan?" As an afterthought she added, "Please?"

After the banker had asked enough questions of her to feel satisfied, he asked her one more. "What do you have for collateral?" He eyed her with a smug look. He had her cornered now. He was sure of it.

"What's dat, co-latt-ral?" she asked with a perplexing look on her face. She was slowly losing more of her gumption. As she began to doubt herself, she wondered if this was a good idea.

The banker knew he had her. "Well, collateral is like property. Do you own something valuable? Like land, a house, or something else like that."

"Oh, jah! I own land. My husband and I homesteaded 160 acres over in Grover township. It's mine now though."

The little man behind the counter looked ever so surprised. "In that case I think we can accommodate you."

Selma thought, "Vat-ever dat 'a-com-o-date' means, he seems happier."

It didn't take long for her to fill out the paperwork and finish the banker's many requests. Before Selma left the bank, she stood and shook his hand.

With her head held high Selma turned and walked past all the remaining men lined up behind her. She tucked the loan money safely in her purse and walked out into the fresh Dakota air.

She had done it. Selma Amanda Dahlgren Sjöqvist had climbed a huge mountain ruled by men. Now she needed to use these precious $100 wisely and eventually pay it all back. There was relief in knowing she had the money in hand, but deciding which bills would take precedence, and eventually paying back the loan were even bigger challenges to conquer. Could she do it? She hoped so. ∞

Document No.

9040

This Mortgage Witnesseth, That _Selma Sjoqvist, a widow_ of _Renville_ County, State of North Dakota, Mortgagor......, in consideration of the sum of _____ _One Hundred and no/100_ _____ DOLLARS, the receipt whereof is hereby acknowledged, do..... hereby Grant, Convey and Mortgage to _The First National Bank of Kenmare, North Dakota_ Mortgagee......, the following described premises, situated in the County of Renville. and State of North Dakota, to-wit:

The West half (W½) of the North east quarter (N E ¼) and East half (E½) of the North West quarter (N W ¼) of Section Twenty eight (28) Township One Hundred Sixty two (162), North of Range Eighty six (86) West of the 5th P. M. containing one hundred sixty (160) acres, more or less, according to the Government survey thereof.

together with all the hereditaments and appurtenances thereunto belonging.

The Mortgagor......hereby covenant....with the Mortgagee.....and assigns, that she _is will_ seized in fee simple of the aforesaid premises; that they are free from all incumbrances except a Mortgage for,.................................... _One Thousand and no/100_ _____ DOLLARS, and that she....will WARRANT and DEFEND the title to the same to the Mortgagee..... and assigns against the lawful claims of all persons whomsoever.

PROVIDED, NEVERTHELESS, That if the Mortgagor......or assigns, shall pay to the Mortgagee.....or assigns, the sum of.................. _One Hundred and no/100_ _____ DOLLARS, with interest thereon, according to the conditions of _three_ promissory note..bearing even date herewith and described as follows, to-wit:

One note for $ _3 0 . 0 0_ ....due _October 15_ 19_13_.   One note for $ _3 0 . 0 0_ ....due _October 15_ 19_14_.
One note for $ _40.00_ ....due _October 15_ 19_15_.   One note for $ ......due....................19......
One note for $ ....due....................19......   One note for $ ......due....................19......

then this Mortgage to be null and void, otherwise to remain in full force and effect. But if default shall be made in the payment of any part of the principal or interest, then the Mortgagee......or assigns, may declare the whole principal sum due and payable, and this Mortgage may be foreclosed at once. And in case of such default the Mortgagee......or assigns......................hereby authorized and empowered to sell the hereby mortgaged premises and convey the same to the purchaser, agreeably to the statute in such case made and provided, and out of the moneys arising from the foreclosure sale, whether said foreclosure be by action or advertisement, to retain the principal and accrued interest, together with all costs and charges and statutory attorney's fees, paying the surplus, if any, to the Mortgagor...... or assigns. And in case of a failure of the Mortgagor...... to pay the taxes, then the Mortgagee......or assigns may pay the same, and such sum shall become a part of this mortgage indebtedness and draw interest at same rate.

IN WITNESS WHEREOF, _I_ ......have hereunto set _my_ hand....and seal..this _15th_ day of _October_ A.D. 1912.

Attest:

P Miller

Don S Riley   _Selma Sjoqvist_

STATE OF NORTH DAKOTA, ss:
County of _Ward_

On this _15th_ day of _October_ A. D. 191_2_, before me personally appeared.................. _Selma Sjoqvist, a widow_

known to me...to be the person who is described in, and who executed the within foregoing instrument, and acknowledged to me that....she......executed the same.

Witness my hand and seal this _15th_ day of _October_ A. D. 1912.

My commission expires _Feb. 8,_ 19_16_.   _Don S Riley Notary Public_
                                            Renville Co. N. D.

OFFICE OF REGISTER OF DEEDS, Renville County, N. D.

Filed in this office for record on the _21_ day of _March_ A. D. 191_3_, at _9_ o'clock _A._M., and was duly recorded in Book _6_ of Mortgages, on page _136_.

By _____ Deputy.   _Walter N Martine_ Register of Deeds.

Note: During the time of farm expansion and settlement, farmers enjoyed fair prices for their wheat. They borrowed money from the banks to increase and/or make additional purchases. By the year 1910 half of all farmers had a mortgage debt. And by 1920 the farms under mortgage were at 71 percent.

Small rural banks depended on grain farmers. Banks were one of the very first business establishments of rural communities. By 1895 North Dakota had 102 banks and by 1910 there were 671. The banks had grown four times faster than the population. Only $10,000 capital was required to establish a bank. The state bank examiner seldom refused an application. Some banks were even opened on entirely borrowed capital.

On August 1, 1899 the Ward County State Bank opened in Kenmare, North Dakota. It had a mere $5,000 in capital. The building had been erected the previous year and stood on the east side of the town square at the corner of Central and Division. When the Ward County State Bank merged with the First National Bank, the entire name of the old bank was dropped and became known as the First National Bank. It remained this way until 1931 when it merged with the Kenmare State Bank and the name was changed to First Kenmare National Bank.

By 1936 the bank was forced to close due to the Great Depression. The bank building is no longer standing today. Another building was erected on the same site and is now occupied by the Farmers Union Insurance.

AN OCEAN BETWEEN

"Wait for the Lord; be strong and take heart and wait for the Lord."

Psalm 27:14

The Hultqvist Home

Prior to 1915

Back in Sweden...

"Is there no end to work?" Ester thought to herself. It wasn't so much a question as it was a thought. "I guess I should just be happy to have a place to live and work. At least I have my little brother with me here. But ..."

Ester rarely finished that sentence. It wouldn't do any good to dream of America and dear, dear Mor. "Will I ever see her or my brothers and sisters again?"

Things had changed for Ester, Erik, and their grandparents. When Mormor and Morfar's health deteriorated, they moved to Nybro. Ester found

Hultqvist Main House (1967)

Mother Hultqvist's Home (1967)

a job working for a family named Hultqvist a short distance away in Algustboda.

When Erik was in school, Ester's mind often drifted away while doing the more mundane daily tasks in the Hultqvist home. She stopped briefly and looked around her. The large Swedish wooden home had a nice-sized kitchen with a built-in stove and oven in one corner of the room. It appeared to be part of the wall because it was made from the same plaster material as the walls themselves. In or-

Mother & Father Hultqvist (1967)

der to keep it neat and clean looking, it required a lot of daily cleaning on Ester's part. Each spring she'd also wash the walls down and then repaint everything white. Although it was work to keep it looking respectable, it was the very best stove for baking bread, cakes, cookies, or other delicious tasting and mouth-watering meals. It could hold the heat with very little wood to fuel the fire.

The rest of the house was especially beautiful. The parlor required only occasional dusting. It was the one room in the house that was seldom opened, except for Christmas, Midsommar, birthdays, holidays, or visitors.

Often when Ester would dust the parlor, she would take time to study the old oval pictures that hung in thick, rectangular frames. They were family photographs of loved ones now long gone. Ester was always extra careful in this room just knowing that all the eyes of so many Hultqvist family members were watching her from the frames on the nearby walls. Beautiful furniture filled the room. The dining table was made of a dark, dense wood. It matched the bureau that held gorgeous dishes, bowls, and other fine pieces of china and Swedish glass. In addition, there were matching chairs with needlepoint seats and a number of shelves holding books of family value. Stuffed chairs around the room provided more comfortable seating.

As Ester would dust, she'd dream that someday, somewhere she'd live in a home this elegant. Maybe, just maybe, she'd get to America, marry some rich Swede, and live happily ever after.

In the meantime there was work to do. As she exited the dignified room, she closed the parlor door. Coming into the kitchen, she took the potatoes she had dug from the garden. Putting them on the kitchen table and getting a paring knife, she sat down on the chair and began to peel the potatoes. The men would be coming in for supper and her little brother would soon be bounding through the door from school. She needed to hurry.

Prior to her job at the Hultqvist home, Ester and Erik had lived in the home of her grandparents, Mormor and Morfar Dahlgren. But time had taken its toll on these two elderly people who loved her and her brother so much. They no longer lived in their old home in Gränö. Instead they had moved to a pensioner complex in Nybro. Here life was a little easier for the two of them. They were close to their church in Madesjö and could attend more frequently or have the minister come to visit them.

Ester smiled to herself as she thought of the love that warmed her heart for these two special people. They had given and given up so much for her

Hultqvist homes (2010)

and her little brother. She was eager to catch a ride into Nybro for a visit. Both she and Erik needed to feel the arms of their grandparents around them in love.

ᔕᗞ ONCE SUPPER DISHES were finished and the Hultqvist children were tucked into bed, Ester took Erik by the hand and climbed the stairs to bed. Her little brother was seven and a half years younger than she and in many ways she had taken the place of his Mor.

Ester was exhausted, but she took time to listen to all the things Erik had to share. This was their special time together. While they sat on the edge of the bed, Ester put her arm around her brother. As she listened to him talk, she stroked his hair across his forehead. He was such a gentle, caring person. His first thoughts were always for others. Whenever he'd come into the house Erik's first question was, "How's your day going?"

After prayers with Erik that night, Ester went to her own bed. But, sleep did not come easily. She lay awake for hours thinking of America. She wondered what her Mor looked like. It had been so many years since Ester had been eight years old, that she could barely remember. Time had removed most of the clear images in her head.

Ester vowed that night to work even harder to get herself and Erik to America. The longing within her was very deep. There was an ache that would never go away until she could lay eyes on her Mor and deliver this darling little brother to the arms of her waiting mother. ∽

Berta Gertrud Viktoria Hultqvist (1906 - 1986) in her kitchen (Midsommar June 1967)

Berta Hultqvist with her married sister, Gullan, and Gullan's husband, Simorn (June 23, 1967)

"There is a time for everything, and a season for every activity under heaven: a time to be born and a time to die, ... a time to weep and a time to laugh, a time to mourn and a time to dance..."

Ecclesiastes 3:1-4

Losses and Gains

1913 - 1915

Devastating news arrived in the fall of 1913. Selma held the letter in her hands as she read her father's words. "My dear daughter. I am so very sorry that I must write you with some very sad news. Your Mor, Maria Helena Jonsson Dahlgren, passed away on October 3rd. The rest of us are fine. Ester and Erik will miss their Mormor, but seem to thrive at the Hultqvist home."

Selma could hardly believe what she was reading. Her mother. How ironic her mother's life ended on October 3rd. It was on this very exact day two years earlier, her husband had died. And now her mother. Selma consoled herself with the thought that Ester could continue to care for Erik. Maybe these two children would still be safe and secure in the home of Ester's work. She remembered the Hultqvist family as kind and good people.

It had been awhile since Ester and Erik had resided with their grandparents. Selma now knew her children's visits with their loving Swedish grandfather would be especially needed for comfort. Not just for him, but also for Ester and Erik.

Selma grieved. Any existing hopes were dashed when a second letter arrived three months after her mother's passing. Selma reached for the closest chair. Her eyes blurred while reading that her father, Johan Dahlgren, was also gone. It had happened on January 8th of 1914. Selma's heart was about to break with grief. She was an only child and now both of her parents were gone. She was an orphan. The finality of it was just so hard to grasp and understand.

What would happen to Ester and Erik? Selma's two children had lost the security and love of their Swedish grandparents. Now what?

Selma searched for her own comfort. She knew her two children would still be able to find solace with each other. But, they were so far away. How she yearned to take them in her arms and give needed assurances. Selma prayed this time would come quickly.

As much as she reasoned and rationalized the happenings of the past few months, Selma refused to give up hope. Somehow things just had to work out right.

When Selma's American children heard the sad news, Herman, John, and Ingeborg knew beyond a shadow of doubt that their meager earnings were of gigantic importance. Every penny, every nickel, and every dime possible, needed to be stashed away to earn ticket passages for their Swedish brother and sister. Frantically they worked to make this happen. These three kids had to grow up fast in an adult world that was not always fair to their young ages. This was true physically and emotionally, but monetarily they were often taken advantage of with wages that would be unacceptable by older adults.

On the other side of the ocean Ester was also desperately working. She worked tirelessly for the Hultqvist family of parents, daughters, and son Hugo. The entire family loved Ester and her hard work ethics. They felt her deep sorrow in the loss of her grandparents.

Like her brothers and sister across the ocean, Ester was putting away every krona possible. She needed enough to purchase tickets to America for both herself and her little brother, Erik.

It was a joyous day in 1915 when money earned on both sides of the vast ocean was added together to purchase passage to North Dakota. Ester counted and recounted, "There is enough, Erik! We've got enough to go to America!!"

Happiness on the United States side was equally expressed. The entire Sjöqvist family was ecstatic as they danced around the homestead living room.

ᔕ FOR THE FIRST LEG of the journey, Ester Gunhild Alfrida and Erik Knut Valdemar had to travel from their home in southeast Sweden to Göteborg on the southwest coast, the same way the rest of the family had begun the long journey. By the time they were ready to leave Ester was nineteen years old and Erik was eleven. Over ten years had passed since they had last seen their mother, Selma. And Erik never had a chance to see his Far.

During their time in Göteborg, Ester met another 19-year-old Swedish gal by the name of Olga Katarina Persson. She was traveling with her four-year-old son, Ivar Gowhard and they were also headed for North Dakota. At first Olga thought her destination was the Heimdal/Maddoch area. Later, Ester found out that Olga's friend, Frans Peters or Peterson was now in Roseglen, North Dakota. But it didn't matter exactly where. Ester knew that she would enjoy the friendship of another person accompanying them to the same general area in America.

So, these four newfound friends purchased tickets on February 8, 1915 for the entire trip from Göteborg, Sweden to North Dakota in America. On the next leg of the journey they rode the train to Bergen, Norway. As they rode through the rough and rugged countryside they marveled at the magnificent views of lakes, rivers, fjords, and plenty of mountains. This was the safest and quickest way to get to Bergen. Once in Bergen they would meet the huge steamship that would take them all the way across the Atlantic Ocean.

On February 11, 1915, Ester and Erik were ready to board a 530-foot long ship by the name of *Kristianiafjord*. This was not the largest of vessels

Immigrants on the deck of an Atlantic Liner (1906)
Photo: Edwin Levick

to carry passengers, but it was the most affordable which was important for them. Their tickets were for third class or steerage.

The year 1915 was sandwiched between a number of major events in history. World War I was raging. It was already affecting the waters of northern Europe. England had shut down all passenger ship travel because of the major conflicts of this war. Rumors flew like wildfire and countries lay-in-wait for fear of what could possibly happen next and to whom and where.

The unsinkable Titanic steamship had gone down in April 1912. After losing so many passengers aboard this giant vessel, there was major trepidation on the part of anyone purchasing tickets for crossing the wild Atlantic. This was especially true of the winter months when the seas were the most turbulent. The wild waters, ice chunks and fog at this time of year were hazardous. Ester and Erik were traveling smack dab in the middle of winter. ∞

The *S. S. Kristianiafjord* was built in 1913 by the Cammell Laird and Company in Birkenhead, England. At 530 feet long and 61 feet wide, it weighed 10,669 (gross) tons. It had steam quadruple expansion engines that were twin screw. The service speed could reach fifteen knots. It could carry 1,200 passengers. Of these 100 were first class, 250 were second class, and 850 were third class. It had been built for the Norwegian-America Line. It flew under the Norwegian flag and offered services from Oslo and Bergen to New York.

On July 15, 1917 the *S. S. Kristianiafjord* was shipwrecked off the coast of England.

"Go home to your family and tell them how much the Lord has done for you, and how he has had mercy on you."

Mark 5:19

Will We Know Them?

1915

Ester and Erik held onto each other's hands as they walked onto the Norwegian vessel in Bergen. They had left their home in Gränö and Algustboda in Sweden. They were headed for New York in America. Would their dreams come true at long last?

Both Ester and Erik were excited but guarded. Would their Mor love them the same as when she left over ten years ago? Would their brothers and sisters accept them for whom they had become? What would Ruth and Edwin be like? This sister and brother were American-born siblings. They had only met them through Mor's letters. There were many more questions than answers.

On the Dakota side of the ocean the family had similar nagging doubts. Neighbors consistently told Selma, "Your two Swedish children will never fit into the family."

The Sjöqvist children would come home with comments they heard at school, work, and in the community. "Your brother and sister will be like strangers to all of you."

Upon hearing these negative statements, Selma gathered her children together. With seriousness in her voice and joy in her heart, she told her children, "Ester and Erik are your sister and brother. They have the same kind of blood running through them as all of you do. The same mother and the same father. You may have been separated for over ten years, but you will be more the same than different. Don't listen to what other people say to you. Just praise our Almighty God that He is making this wonderful day possible."

"Wait right here, children," Selma said as she went to the trunk that held all their important documents. Coming back with a paper, she held it for all of them to see. She proceeded to explain, "On October 2, 1908, your father and I became naturalized citizens of this great land. In addition, this included all of you. Even Ester and Erik." Selma pointed to each of their names on the paper. "So, even though they have been living in Sweden, in reality they have been U.S. citizens all this time."

Selma stopped for a moment to let it all sink in. "Have no fear. We will all be together once again."

Selma's words brought comfort to her children. They became more confident and eagerly looked forward to the day of their brother and sister's arrival. Ester had written that the *S. S. Kristianiafjord* was expected to arrive in New York on February 20, 1915. They could hardly wait. ☜

"Though my father and mother forsake me, the LORD will receive me. I am still confident of this: I will see the goodness of the LORD in the land of the living."
Psalm 27:10, 13

Ellis Island

1915

On February 20, 1915 the Norwegian *S. S. Kristianiafjord* pulled into the New York harbor. The oceanliner headed for a pier on Manhattan's east side. Ester and Erik watched as first- and second-class passengers disembarked. Because they were third class, they had been instructed to stay on board the vessel. Before leaving the large steamship they would be tagged with proper identification.

Once tagged, Ester and Erik boarded a smaller boat. They watched as the little vessel passed by the gigantic city of New York. While on the journey they had heard others talk about this very large city. Now they believed it to be true as they watched the tall buildings, houses, boats on the water's

Second Ellis Island
Immigration Station
opened on
December 17, 1900

Photo: A. Coeffler, 1905

edge and an endless shoreline pass in front of them. They could only imagine all the people living so close together.

Ester and Erik were in awe at what they saw next. It was a statue of a tall lady holding a torch high above her head. They couldn't imagine what it was all about. Just then Ester's friend Olga came closer as she held Ivar's hand. "The man over there just told me that we were passing by the Statue of Liberty. She's holding a torch as a sign of welcome." The four young people looked around and noticed that everyone on board was absolutely silent. Even the babies had hushed their crying. The whole group was mesmerized in total silence. Ester took Erik's hand as they gazed at the giant figure in the distance. After passing, the two moved closer to Olga and little Ivar.

"Uffda! I've never seen anything like that before," said Ester, as she continued to search through the haze for one last look.

It didn't take long until the boat arrived at Ellis Island. Before anyone would be allowed to proceed on to their destinations, they would need to pass through the dreaded immigration inspection.

After the boat docked Ester, Erik, Olga, and Ivar lugged their belongings to the entry level. It felt strange and yet good to step down on solid ground. They were excited to have gotten this far and yet petrified of the upcoming immigration procedure.

As the four entered the Great Hall to start the inspection process, they stopped and looked around. The hall had hundreds and hundreds of people milling about. They were filled with trepidation over the unknown that lay before them. This was a frightening time for anyone and especially for young people unfamiliar with travel. In addition to the chaos of so many people being pushed and prodded along, they heard various languages spoken all around them. But, other than Norwegian and Swedish, they understood little if anything.

Immigrants gaze on the Statue of Liberty, a gift from France that was dedicated October 28, 1886

New immigrants from various countries waiting in line at Ellis Island

In all of Ester's 19 years and Erik's 11 years, they had never been this far away from home. But where was home anyway? Was it in their native Sverige, the land they had just left? Or was it America and the Dakota home where their mother, brothers, and sisters lived?

Putting these questions aside, Ester focused on the path that lay before her. She was a "take charge" young woman, a skill she had learned early in life while helping her grandparents care for her little brother.

Ester grabbed Erik's hand and held tight. She warned him, "Don't let go. No matter what. Ok?" *How would they ever find each other again if they were separated?*

It was scary to say the least. Ester needed to be the responsible one of the two, but worries and fears nagged at her. What if they did get separated? What if they couldn't understand the immigration officials? What would happen if they didn't pass all the inspections? What if? What if?

While all of Ester's senses were on high alert, Erik was much more laid back. He was used to taking orders from his big sister. He would never think of not following her directions. Besides that, he felt secure whenever Ester was in charge.

Ester had heard that men and women, boys and girls were separated once they entered the huge immigration building. It was with high anxiety that Ester hung on desperately to Erik's hand.

After standing in line for what seemed like forever, Ester could see it would soon be her turn to answer questions. Stepping up to the inspector, Ester noted that his name tag read, "Frank Macatee." Looking up from his papers, he asked, "What is your name?"

Ester stared at the man and wondered what he had just said. Then she remembered the tag pinned to her coat. She pointed to the tag and he nodded back at her. After checking all the paperwork and giving them each a quick examination, Mr. Macatee stamped "SI" on the Alien Manifest to the left of their names. They didn't understand this meant "Special Inquiry."

As a result Ester and Erik were put into still another line. Not aware of the magnitude of what just happened to them, Ester found some comfort when Olga and Ivar joined this same line.

After another long wait, a doctor came and checked their eyes, looked down their throats, and examined each of them more thoroughly. By 10:30 a.m., Mr. Macatee stamped "Admitted to Hospital" after Ester's name.

Ester still didn't know what all this meant, but she continued to hang tightly onto Erik's hand. She only relaxed her hold somewhat when the authorities made her understand that Erik could remain with her. "We'll be okay now, Erik." Her words were meant to comfort him, but they were also reassuring to herself as well.

Olga and little Ivar were examined a second time and admitted into the country without further detention. Ester looked back as she was escorted away. She caught Olga's eyes. Instantly the girls understood the dire situation. Hesitantly, Olga raised her hand in the slightest of waves. Ester never raised her hand in reply as the tears streamed unchecked down her face. She had absolutely no idea why Olga got to go and she had to stay.

Turning back to watch where she was going, Ester focused on what lay before them. She gripped Erik's hand firmly as she gave him an ever so slight smile of reassurance.

Day after day, doctors and nurses examined and re-examined Ester. The days drug on and with each passing day Ester's fears mounted. Would she ever be released? What if they were sent back to Sweden? Wouldn't Mor be frantic by now?

The one thing that kept them going each day was the yearning to see the mother, brothers, and sister that had left them many years before. They were also eager to meet their unknown little sister, Ruth, and youngest brother, Edwin. Ester could almost feel her loving mother's arms around her. It would never be too soon.

The Great Hall at Ellis Island

In order to pass the time, Ester related stories to young Erik about his unknown and long-forgotten family. She told him about the father he had never met. Upon hearing the wonderful happenings of their Far, Erik silently grieved for this giant of a man he would never know. He had missed out on so much in their family separation.

Ester told him of his big brothers, Herman and John. He also learned about his big sister, Ingeborg. And as he listened, he learned to know them through her tales and he looked forward to meeting them.

But the one thing that always brought tears to his sister's eyes was when Ester spoke of their mother, Selma. Her voice changed and love radiated from her face. It took a lot for Ester to get choked up over anything. She was always in charge of things, especially her emotions. Erik knew that this woman, his Mor, must be someone very, very special.

On the nineteenth day of hospitalization Ester had her breakfast like usual. Erik watched her as she ate and enjoyed his own food as well. She had no more finished eating her hot cereal and coffee, when the doctor entered her room. Each time that she was examined, Ester trembled with deep inner fear. Would this ordeal never, ever end?

Her mouth fell open when the doctor looked her in the eyes and asked, "Would you like to be on your way today?" It took a few moments for the interpreter to explain what the doctor meant.

"Can I? Can we? I mean, yes! Yes!!"

"Ok. Let's get you on your way to North Dakota." Turning to the nurse, he added. "Ester Sjöqvist is being discharged today. Would you get her paperwork accomplished and tell Frank Macatee to stamp "Discharged" on Ester's papers. Also, have him stamp "Admitted" over the "SI" on both her and her brother's paperwork. Then these two can be on their way!"

By one o'clock in the afternoon all the paperwork was done. Ester had eaten her last meal at Ellis Island and she and Erik had spent their last night.

One of the immigration volunteers offered to assist the two with their luggage. They also helped them in securing the railway tickets they'd need for the final leg of their journey.

The tickets had been purchased at Göteborg, but with the long detention at Ellis Island, changes needed to be made.

The two finally relaxed as the train pulled away from the station and Ester let go of Erik's hand. She leaned over and hugged him. Then the two burst out laughing! "Here we go!" Eric shouted. ∽

RECORD OF ALIENS HELD FOR SPECIAL INQUIRY.

S. S. Kristianiafjord (Norw. Amer.) arrived February 20, 1915, 191_ M., _____ from _____ 104 ✓

		NAME.	MANIFEST. Sheet No.			CAUSE OF DETENTION.	Inspector.	ACTIONS OF THE BOARDS OF SPECIAL INQUIRY. Disc.—Exc.	Reconsider.	Admitted.		DEPARTMENTAL AND EXECUTIVE ORDER. Date. Excl. Conced.	DEPORTED. Date. Ship.	MEALS.
22a	1	Axness, Marcus	5	5	1	LPC Immoral Purposes 13.40 Scarlett				2/21 91 & 10⁰⁰				1 1 ✓
22a	2	Baldy, Kora	9	5	1	12.40 "				2/21 91 & 10⁰⁰				1 1 ✓
19a	3	Dseler, Hialmer	7	25	1	1.30 Tierney	2/25 99 Nw 7/3 14		2/26 11.22 an					12.11 7/3
28a	4	Aun, Christian	5	1	1	1.55 Ross			2/25 09 & 11⁰⁰					3 3 3
19f	5	Loquist, Ester	27 18/16	2		Dischg 3/10 10-30 Released 3/10 PM 1.45 Koester	2/25 09 Lou		3 10 an 1⁰⁰					19 19 19
19a		" Erik												
19a	6	Loquist, Daniel O.	11	5	1	LPC 1.90 Ross	2/25 09 Lou		2/26 11 & 4⁴⁵					7 2 2
19a	7	Anderson, Adolf Gustaf	6	5	1	" 1.55	2/26 111 Lou		2/26 112 2					4 4 4
15a	8	Sellberg, Nils Johan	7 18/21	5		1.45 Tierney			2/26 110 Lou 2 & 65					★
15a		" Gustav Ed												
8a		" Anna M.												
14a	9	Johannsson, Gustav Al.	24	25	1	LPC 2.00 Schw.	2/26 8 & 7/3		2/26 116 & 12 80					15 4 5
26f	10	Nilsihmsen, Henriette	7	26		" 2.10 Tierney			2/26 115 Lou &					
16a	11	Andreasen, Andreas M.	25	1	1	2.00 Marm	2/26 115 Lou		2/26 29 & 10 80					3 2 3
19f	12	Persson, Olga V.	26 18/19	5		2.30 Schw.			2/26 117 Lou 8 & 65					

Note: Only legal papers were retained by Ellis Island officials. According to the government, hospital papers were not considered legal papers and were destroyed. Therefore, the reason and details of Ester's stay are unknown. We do know that she was admitted on February 21, 1915 at 10:30 a.m. Ester and Erik each ate nineteen breakfasts, dinners, and suppers. Ester was released on March 10, 1915 at 1:00 p.m.

Researchers at Ellis Island stated that Ester and Erik could have been detained for reasons other than medical issues. People entering the country were expected to bring money. An amount of $20 was acceptable, but $25 was preferred. Ester claimed $1 and Erik had $0. Immigration officials also refused to send single women into the country alone. Therefore, unescorted women and children were detained with immigrants having medical issues, and kept until their safety was assured through the arrival of a telegram, a letter, a prepaid ticket, or money from waiting relatives. Ester and Erik had prepaid tickets to their final destination. Once a letter and money arrived, a Special Inquiry hearing was held with the board of inspectors. Whatever the reason was for detention, after 19 days Ester and Erik were discharged and admitted into the country.

The first two lines of #5 indicate Ester & Erik with the last name of "Loquist" Olga Persson is listed on line 12

"Blessed are those who dwell in your house; they are ever praising you."
Psalm 84:4

Together Again

March 15, 1915

T he train just couldn't go fast enough to suit these two travelers. The extremely long and difficult journey was finally nearing its end. Soon, Ester and Erik would be in Tolley, North Dakota.

Ester once again took Erik's hand. The closer they got, the harder she squeezed it. The two were so excited, Ester was certain everyone could see their hearts beating out of their chests. "We're pulling into the station! We're here! We're here!"

Back row: Ingeborg, Selma, Ester; *Front row*: Erik, Ruth (March 15, 1915)

Early in the morning hours of March 15, 1915, it all came true. All expectations were met and all fears melted away the minute Erik and Ester entered the Sjöqvist home. Tears flowed freely. Everyone talked at once. There was joy in bountiful measure.

Selma could not take her eyes off her two Swedish, yet naturalized, American children. Her wildest and most remote dreams had at last come true.

These children were so grown up now. Ester was a young woman and Erik, who had been a one-year-old baby when she left him, was now a tall and slender lad. He was soft and kind with a gentle nature. She couldn't have been more happy.

That night when everyone was tucked into bed, Selma went to the throne of God in prayer. She praised God's abundant mercy and goodness. She thanked Him over and over again. Tears streamed down her face. When she was about finished, Selma raised her face heavenward. "Oh God, if there is ever a way, could you just let Johan have a glimpse of his family now? He would be so proud." ∽

Ester on the day she arrived at the homestead, March 15, 1915

A son and daughter of Mrs. Selma Sjorquist arrived Monday morning from Sweden.

Newspaper clipping in *The Tolley Journal*, Friday, March 19, 1915

"The troubles of my heart have multiplied; free me from my anguish. Look upon my affliction and my distress and take away all my sins."

Psalm 25:17-18

My Little Son

April 1915

Selma's excitement of having all seven of her children under one roof was a mother's dream come true. Could it really be possible? She was elated as she watched the small group reconnect in a way that only seven brothers and sisters could.

For the first time after arriving from Sweden, Ester and Erik met their little sister, Ruth, and younger brother, Edwin. Ruth danced around the house like she was the "belle-of-the-ball." She loved all the attention that was lavished on her. Her excitement could not be contained.

Edwin was the opposite. He was a quiet and reserved seven year old. He was tall for his age and had a strong desire to grow up to the height of his big brothers, Herman, John, and now Erik.

Edwin would sit and watch all the antics of his big brothers and sisters. Eventually, one by one, they would approach him and draw him into conversation and play. The one thing that did excite him was his upcoming birthday. He was counting the days in eager anticipation of his special day, May 6.

About ten days after the arrival of her two Swedish children, Selma noticed that Edwin was especially quiet and even more reserved than usual. As a mother, she was on high alert for changes noted in her children.

The Tolley Journal, January 22, 1915 (showing perfect attendance)

> The pupils of school No. 2 neither tardy nor absent the past month are: Reuben Johnson, Johney Knutson, Bertha and Nels Olson, Edvin and Ruth Sjoqvist and Wilbert Schweitzer.

Finding a time when her little son was alone, she approached him in his bed after the others were off to sleep.

"What's the matter, son?" she inquired. While asking, she placed her hand on his forehead. He was warm to the touch.

"I'm ok," was his quick reply. "But my throat hurts a little."

"Maybe, you should stay home from school tomorrow."

"But I want to go. Please," he begged.

Edwin was not a child that demanded attention or ever asked for much. And so, Selma relented and sent him off with Ruth in the direction of school the next day.

Later in the day when the children arrived home from school, she noted that Edwin appeared very flushed. When Selma felt his forehead, he was hot to the touch. She watched as he trembled with chills after removing his coat and cap.

"It's to bed with you," she ordered. "I have something nice and hot for that sore throat."

When Selma came to his bedside with some hot broth, she found her little son fast asleep.

"Maybe he needs rest more than he needs nourishment."

Edwin never awoke until morning. Selma had already sent the others on their way in various directions. Only Ester had remained behind.

Ester came to her mother. "Mor, Edwin is burning up, has chills that won't stop, and he can't stop crying. What should we do?"

Selma was as touched by the deep concern of her eldest child as she was over the worry of her youngest little son. "We'll see if we can get some broth into him. If he isn't better in a few days we'll have one of the boys go to Tolley and fetch Doctor Critchfield."

Money was always a huge issue for the Sjöqvist family. Retrieving the services of the Tolley doctor would be

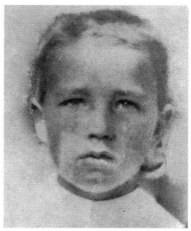

Edwin Sigmund Herbert Sjöqvist, approximately 7 years old

DR. CRITCHFIELD TO LEAVE TOLLEY

Dr. L. R. Critchfield has sold his residence and practice to Dr. Z. P. King of Minneapolis, and will move to Kenmare, where he expects to take up special practice in diseases of ear and throat. Dr. Critchfield, during his stay here, has made many friends who regret to see him leave.

Dr. King is a native of Minnesota and a graduate of the University of Minnesota and was for a time Assistant Police Surgeon, and later for eighteen months House Surgeon in the City Hospital, Minneapolis, and has had four months experience in American Ambulance Service in France. He is a man of pleasing personality and comes to us well recommended.

Critchfield followed Rainville and Dallager as area doctors. *The Tolley Journal* newspaper reported his leaving (August 11, 1916).

another need requiring cash that was meager and difficult to come by. But, she had never seen any of her children this sick either.

By the twelfth day Edwin's condition had worsened. His temperature was even higher and he went in and out of coherency. He was unable to keep any liquids down.

On April 6 the doctor was sent for from Tolley. He arrived as quickly as possible. He was always on the run, visiting the sick, and delivering new babies throughout the Tolley area.

His concern over Edwin's condition was never revealed by his facial expressions. After a thorough examination, he turned to Selma. "He has a very severe case of tonsillitis. It will be important that we bring the fever down. Put cold compresses on him and bathe him with cool to lukewarm water. I'll check back with you."

Following the doctor's orders, Selma and her two oldest daughters, Ester and Ingeborg, worked around the clock to lower little Edwin's temperature. They took turns through the night, bathing him and putting cold compresses on his forehead.

Edwin, less than a year old, with mother Selma

They kept this vigil up until Dr. Critchfield returned days later. Edwin appeared somewhat better at times. They could get his temperature down, but in a matter of minutes it would return to new heights. This time the doctor gave Selma some medicine. "When his temperature goes down, try to get him to take some of these. I'll check again in a couple of days."

And so, the vigilance continued. Edwin took the medication and kept it down for a short period of time. Then all of a sudden all liquids, broth, and drugs were expelled.

Selma could see how weak Edwin was becoming. And yet, Selma kept her thoughts to herself as she continued to nurse her child day after day and hour after hour. Even when exhausted and her daughters insisted she get some rest, sleep seemed to elude her. Instead she lay on her bed with her eyes closed as she petitioned God to intervene. She'd roll on her side with her back to her children as tears coursed down her face.

Edwin at times over the next few days did appear to be improving. Once they even got him to sit up for a few minutes. His cough was deep and hacking. Occasionally, he spit up blood after a coughing siege. His color was pasty white.

After being sick for over three weeks, Edwin's flesh color took on a yellowish tinge. When the doctor examined him this time, he was unable to mask his deep concern. Edwin's condition was deteriorating. Things did not look good. "He's having a lot of trouble. His liver and kidneys are having a hard time working. Keep him comfortable and keep praying."

Edwin, at about two years old

The Sjöqvist family sat around his bedside. Selma pleaded to God to save her little boy's life. He was the baby of the family and held a special place in her heart. Edwin was her gentle child. He was the one that could make her laugh. He held her last "love connection" with her Johan.

On about the 28th day Selma awoke from a frightful sleep. She heard a deep rattling cough coming from her youngest child. She listened momentarily to his labored breathing. Immediately, she was on her feet and at her child's bedside.

Edwin's fever was back with a vengeance. He would get spells of coughing that just wouldn't stop. She immediately recognized it as pneumonia. This was the very thing she dreaded, especially with Edwin's weakened condition and his failing heart, kidneys, and liver.

In the wee hours of the morning, as each of her children entered the kitchen she said the same thing, "I want you all to stay home today. Edwin has taken a turn for the worse and we'll need to be here together."

"What can we do to help?" each of them asked.

"Go sit with him and encourage him to keep fighting. Talk to him. Sing. Tell him you love him. But, most importantly, PRAY."

During the next few hours, they did just as their mother had told them. Ester and Erik told about Sweden and their trip across the ocean. Herman told about the neighbors that he was working for. John played his violin. Ingeborg and Ruth told him countless times how much they loved him. And, all of them prayed with earnest devotion.

The doctor came and stayed with them. There was little now that even he could do.

At about ten o'clock in the morning with Selma holding her youngest son, Edwin Sigmund Herbert Sjöqvist, died.

It was April 22, 1915 and Edwin was two weeks shy of his eighth birthday. Selma's children had all been together for only five weeks. The doctor shook his head as he wrote seven years, eleven months, and fourteen days old on the death certificate.

As Selma had watched the life ebb out of her little child, she searched for answers. "Why had God made it possible for her to have her two children returned to her from Sweden only to allow this, her youngest, to be taken from her? Why? Oh, why?" ∽

Note: Penicillin was discovered in 1928 and came to be used during the 1940s. There was limited medical help available in the form of drugs in 1915.

"Children of the Heavenly Father"

A Swedish Lutheran Hymn; Words: Karolina W. Sandell-Berg, 1858
Translated from Swedish to English: Ernst W. Olson in *The Hymnal*, 1925.

Children of the heavenly Father
Safely in His bosom gather;
Nestling bird nor star in Heaven
Such a refuge e'er was given.

Lo, their very hairs He numbers,
And no daily care encumbers
Them that share His ev'ry blessing
And His help in woes distressing.

Though He giveth or He taketh,
God His children ne'er forsaketh;
His the loving purpose solely
To preserve them pure and holy.

Neither life nor death shall ever
From the Lord His children sever;
Unto them his grace He showeth,
And their sorrows all He knoweth.

God His own doth tend and nourish;
In His holy courts they flourish;
From all evil things He spares them;
In His mighty arms He bears them.

Praise the Lord in joyful numbers:
Your Protector never slumbers.
At the will of your Defender
Ev'ry foeman must surrender.

"Blessed is the man who perseveres under trial, because when he has stood the test, he will receive the crown of life that God has promised to those who love him."
James 1:12

Another Loss

1915

Selma's emotions were flung from the pinnacle of happiness to the depths of despair within a few short weeks. Her tears of happiness had been replaced with tears of grief.

There were so many dreaded illnesses that descended on early pioneers. There were flu epidemics, scarlet fever, and diphtheria to name a few. North Dakota, including Grover Township, was no exception. With each obstacle in front of her, Selma Sjöqvist dug deeper to restore her soul.

It was on a cool Saturday, April 24, 1915, when Selma laid her second family member to rest in the soil of North Dakota. She found comfort knowing little Edwin would be close to his father, Johan. The cemetery that had been created at McKinney now held both of her loved ones. They were wrapped together in the rich dirt by a loop of the gentle flowing Mouse River Valley.

Even though Edwin was not yet eight years old, he had known the important significance of the reunited family. He had felt the crisis of the separation by the vast ocean between Sweden and America. He had also known the joys of meeting his big sister and brother for the first time.

Selma's refuge was in these very thoughts. As she beseeched God for peace and support, she also thanked God that He had spared the rest of the family.

The Sjöqvist family clung desperately to each other and their continued faith in a loving God. With each new trial, Selma's faith provided strength. Each day she wanted to curl up and never get out of bed, but instead she arose and put one foot in front of the other with an inner ferocity. It was a strength Selma didn't know she even had within her. As a result she became resilient in her quiet and determined nature. Somehow, someway, she would survive and rise above even this. She had to. Her family was depending on her for leadership now more than ever.

"God help me!" was her daily prayer. ∽

Edwin Sjorquist

Edwin, the eight year old boy of Mrs. Selma Sjorquist, living north of town, died Wednesday night of complications. The little lad had not been well for the past month and recently contracted pneumonia. This together with a weak heart proved the little one's undoing and the end came late Wednesday night with very little suffering. Funeral arrangements are as yet not completed but it is expected to take place tomorrow (Saturday) afternoon, Rev. Gulleen officiating.

The Tolley Journal,
Friday, April 23, 1915

Note: There is a discrepancy on the time of Edwin's death. The newspaper obituary states that he died in the evening. The death certificate states it occurred at 10 am. The writer used the time stated on the death certificate because it was filed by Dr. Critchfield with Selma (mother) assisting.

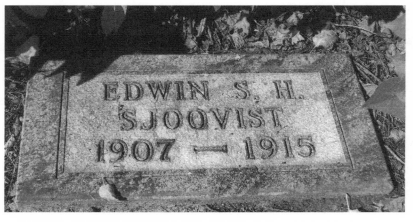

Edwin Sigmund Herbert Sjöqvist was born on May 6, 1907.

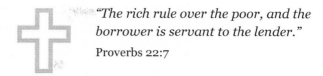

"The rich rule over the poor, and the borrower is servant to the lender."
Proverbs 22:7

Pay Up or Else

October 23, 1918

Selma was hard at work in her farmstead home when she heard footsteps followed by a knock. She stopped her cleaning and quickly opened the door. In front of her stood a tall gentleman wearing something shiny.

"May I help you?" she inquired.

"Hello. My name is Martin H. Haugan and I'm the sheriff of Renville County." He stopped and looked down at the paper in his hands. "Are you Mrs. Selma Sjöqvist?"

"Yah. Dat's me."

He looked at her with deep concern. "I'm ever so sorry, madam, but I've been sent here to deliver this paper."

Selma softly inquired, "And, vat paper is dat? I really don't know vat it is dat you are talking about."

"This is a foreclosure notification." As he handed her the paper he added, "I'm sorry, madam, but you haven't paid your loan and now your homestead will be put up for sale." After tipping his hat he abruptly turned and left.

Taking the paper in her hand Selma immediately recognized the doom of the situation. Selma's property would be sold in a foreclosure sale in Mohall on December 7, 1918. Buyers were to gather on the front steps of the courthouse at two o'clock in the afternoon and the property would be sold to the highest bidder.

Selma watched as the sheriff left the yard. Then she momentarily took a few steps forward and surveyed her yard, fields, treed coulees, and her

NOTICE OF REAL ESTATE MORT-GAGE FORECLOSURE SALE

Notice is hereby given that that certain mortgage, executed and delivered by Selma Sjoquist, a widow, Mortgagor, to The First National Bank of Kenmare, North Dakota, a corporation, Mortgagee dated the 15th day of October, 1912, and filed for record in the office of the Register of Deeds of Renville County, North Dakota, on the 21st day of March, 1913 at 9 o'clock A. M., and duly recorded in Book "6" of Mortgages at Page "136", will be foreclosed by a sale of the premises in such mortgage and hereinafter described at the front door of the Courthouse in the City of Mohall, County of Renville, and State of North Dakota, at the hour of two (2:00) o'clock P. M., on the 7th day of December, 1918, to satisfy the amount due on said mortgage on the date of sale.

The premises described in such mortgage and which will be sold to satisfy the same are described as follows:

West Half (W½) Northeast Quarter (NE¼) and East Half (E½) of the Northwest Quarter (NW¼) of Section Twenty-eight (28) Township One Hundred Sixty-two (162) North of Range Eighty-six (86) West of the Fifth P. M., containing 160 acres more or less according to the government survey thereof.

There will be due on such mortgage on the date of sale the sum of One Hundred Sixty-one and 44-100 ($161.44) Dollars, together with costs of sale.

Dated at Kemare, N. D., this 23d day of October, 1918.

FIRST NATIONAL BANK,
of Kenmare, North Dakota,
P. M. CLARK, Mortgagee.
Attorney for Mortgagee,
Kenmare, N. Dak. (Nl-d6)

The Tolley Journal November 1, 8, 15, 22, 29, and December 6 of 1918

wonderful winding river. Her mind wandered to all that had happened since Johan's death.

❦ SHE REMEMBERED SECURING the bank loan in 1912 for the sum total of $100. During the years following her bank excursion she was supposed to fulfill one payment on October 15, 1913 for $30, another on October 15, 1914 for $30, and the final payment on October 15, 1915 for $40.

What would appear like a small amount to a few of her neighbors, became out of reach for her. From 1912 until 1915 many other things took precedence. Selma's children both in Grover and Sweden had needs that far outweighed her own wishes.

So many factors prevented Selma from making the three promissory note payments. Using her borrowed money to pay taxes, passageway for Ester and Erik to come to North Dakota, and little Edwin's doctor bills had eaten up the bulk of it. In addition to these expenditures, Selma still had unpaid expenses from Johan's doctoring. Each repayment became insurmountable.

Oh, Selma's every fiber desired to pay the money each year. It was like a heavy weight across her shoulders. Each and every time she'd scrape together a few dollars, some need took precedence over the loan payment.

Selma's savings were depleted and she was back to zero. Selma placed all her hopes in a good fall harvest. Maybe then. Just maybe.

The weather elements did not cooperate with Selma's wishes. The rains did not occur in a timely fashion and so the grain kernels shriveled up on their stalks. There was little harvest for any local farmers.

Auction sales became common and neighbors moved away. Still Selma prayed for some form of a happy outcome. She hung onto the farmstead with every raw fiber within her.

In 1916 and 1917 the same weather patterns persisted. Rain was held at bay. The ground was parched and dry. The kernels that did form, eventually dried up without fully developing.

More families sold out and moved from the area. Farm auctions became even more common. The newspapers were filled with foreclosure sales. Still, Selma hung on to hope and her deep faith in an almighty God as she prayed for a miracle.

The year of 1918 was a different story. The rains came down in a timely fashion and the crops once again flourished. The whole surrounding rural community was jubilant with new hope born with each raindrop descending. While wheat prices remained at an all time low, the bountiful crop gave Selma hope.

During this same year, the Spanish Influenza raged throughout the country. The Tolley area had entire families wiped out and many others were under the dreaded quarantine. Selma prayed that she and her children would be spared.

To compound her worries, Selma would be missing the able assistance of her eldest son, Herman. In August he had been drafted into the army. It was World War I and the United States had entered the war against Germany. Many young men were being called up for service. The harvest would be difficult without Herman guiding the hands of his younger siblings.

All hope was crushed when a hailstorm passed through the area. The bountiful crops lay beaten and bruised on the ground. Harvest seemed futile. It would cost more for the harvesters to take the crop off than what could be rendered from the effort. Selma found it difficult to pay the taxes, saying nothing of her dreams of ever paying off the bank loan.

₞ REENTERING HER HOME she closed the door quietly, crossed the room, and sat in the closest chair in the kitchen. She was defeated. This land that she and Johan had homesteaded would soon be gone. This house, her home, was the very place where her husband and youngest child had departed from this world.

Selma lay her head down on her arms resting on the table. She wept. ∞

Note: North Dakota farmers began to struggle during the period of 1914 to 1919. The wheat crops were extremely poor during half of these years. For four straight years the western two-thirds of the state had little precipitation. The year 1917 was the driest on record since North Dakota became a state in 1889.

When inflation hit, it hit hard. The value of land depreciated and wheat prices dropped severely. In addition, North Dakota banks suffered. Many farmers and early homesteaders lost their land and numerous banks failed.

North Dakota banks made loans to farmers far beyond the bounds of good decision making. Banks were advised not to make loans beyond 60 percent of their deposits. Disregarding this recommendation, banks loaned 120 to 285 percent of deposits, with national banks usually on the higher end. Three-fourths of their assets were loans. The banks had very little cash reserve. Thus as the deposits declined during this lean period the banks had no choice, but to collect on their loans to farmers. If the banks failed to collect, the banks failed.

In 1912 there were 587 state banks and by 1917 the number had grown to 701 banks. Within eight years from this date many banks had closed and the number drastically dropped to 494 banks. Throughout these eight years banks struggled to recover and come to grips with the shifting economy. North Dakota suffered greatly. Farmers lost their land, banks failed, and tenancy increased. There was very little optimism.

The early years before 1915 had seen a rapid growth of population. After this period people began to leave North Dakota. Free land was gone. The future turned from the farm to the city. Thus, the greatest export became its own people. More were leaving than were coming in.

World War I drew young men into the military with the first draft on September 5, 1917. The peak number drafted came in May, June, and July of 1918. Young North Dakota men were taken from their farm work and thrust into military action. Sons left the farm and fathers searched for sufficient help. Young women and younger boys were often called upon to fill the gap.

This was the financial situation that caught Selma in its mighty fist. No one had money to purchase her land, the crops failed to produce, her oldest son was drafted into the military, the family's needs took precedence, AND late in 1918 the First National Bank of Kenmare foreclosed on her Grover homestead.

MAP OF GROVER TOWNSHIP

Scale 1¾ inches to 1 mile

Township 162 North, Range 86 West of the 5th P.M.

The Standard Atlas of Renville County North Dakota, page 32; Geo. A. Ogle & Co., 1914.

Going Once, Going Twice

December 7, 1918

As Martin H. Haugan left the homestead of Selma Sjöqvist in Grover Township he felt all kinds of emotions. He was angry, sad, and both physically and emotionally upset with what he had just done. He had accomplished his task, but taking a foreclosure notice to a widow with six children left him with a pit in his stomach.

Often Martin had wanted to leave his job and what he had just done today was the very thing he hated the most. Being a sheriff was not what it was cracked up to be. He had been elected over four years earlier in the fall of 1913. Oh, he still got to wear his shiny badge, but inside he felt dirty, bruised and battered. His heart was no longer in this job. He wanted out.

The upcoming election was being held in November. He truly believed it was time to turn over the reins to his deputy, George A. Scofield. After today he knew that he was more than ready.

George would do a good job. Martin had worked with him since 1914. The two had been together for almost four years now. And so with peace in his heart he resolved that his mind was made up.

∞ THE ELECTION WENT AS Martin had surmised and the new sheriff for Renville County would be George A. Scofield. Now all Martin had to do was bide his time. But that was not really true. The foreclosure sale on the Sjöqvist homestead would be held on December 7, 1918. He was still the official sheriff of the county until the turn of the new year.

Six notices were placed in *The Tolley Journal*. The Sjöqvist foreclosure sale notice was published in the Friday papers on November 1, 8, 15, 22, 29, and December 6.

There was no doubt that the entire neighborhood knew. Martin hoped for a quick and clean sale. The sooner the better would suit him fine. He knew that the First National Bank of Kenmare had every right to attempt to recoup their losses. But...

It had been advertised that the 160-acre homestead would be sold for $161.44 plus all costs of the sale. Hopefully the highest bidder would have money in hand and the sale would end promptly.

On Saturday, December 7, 1918 Martin Haugan exited the Renville County Courthouse and stood at the front doors. It was two o'clock and time for the sale to commence. He noticed only a handful of people present. Most were bank officials along with a few of Mrs. Sjöqvist's neighbors.

Noticing the Sjöqvist friends present, Martin had hope that the sale would perhaps end well for this widow and her children. No matter how hard he tried, he just couldn't shake the last image he had of the woman standing in the doorway of her homestead house. Secretly he'd admired this lady with her fierce determination to somehow succeed even when everything around her was crumbling.

Martin shook these feelings from his mind. This sale had to proceed whether he liked it or not.

Addressing the small group of people standing before him, he an-

Officials and employees in front of the Renville County Courthouse, 1917. (*The Renville County History Book*, page 19, copyright 1976)

nounced that this would be a sale of 160 acres. It included the west half of the northeast quarter and the east half of the northwest quarter of section 28, township 162, north of range 86 and west of the fifth principal meridian.

℘   LATER MARTIN WAS HEARD to tell others, "I first offered the land in separate and legal subdivisions of 40-, 80- and 120-acre tracts."

"What happened?" he was asked.

"Everyone just stood there. I received no bids."

"Then what?"

"Well, I then offered all of the land in one parcel and tract. I wrote in the official book, 'I struck off and sold to and for the price aforesaid.'"

"Who bought it?"

Martin answered slowly, "None of the widow's friends wanted any part of the sale. They looked totally saddened and somewhat disgusted. Finally, it was sold to the Mohall State Bank. I guess that really surprised me too."

"What did it go for?" they pressed.

"The Mohall State Bank paid $210.71. This included the $25 attorney fee, the $13.42 newspaper ads, my fee of $5.60, a $5.00 recording fee for certificates and affidavits, and a 25 cent charge for revenue stamps."

℘   MARTIN H. HAUGAN HAD COMPLETED one of his last duties as Sheriff of Renville County. He was glad it was over.

Mohall State Bank
(approximately 1920)

Martin looked down at his shoes and then raising his head gazed into the faces of his questioners. "I sold the land, but I don't know what Widow Sjöqvist is going to do now. Maybe she'll have her home for the time being."

Before turning to leave, Martin added solemnly, "It is the thing that I pray for now. She absolutely needs a place to live. Let's hope she can at least live in her own home for awhile." ↄ

Note: The value of Selma's $100 loan today (2015) would be approximately $3,000. If you consider the price of gold in 1912 with the price of gold today, it would total $5,100.

In 1918, baths at the barber shop were 35 cents, shoes $1.50 to $2.50, sewing thread 3 cents, ladies shirt waists for 89 cents, beef at 6 cents a pound, hogs at 8 cents a pound, and cars were $235 to $595.

A grocery ad in *The Tolley Journal*, February 23, 1912.

*"I wait for your salvation, O LORD,
and I follow your commands."*
Psalm 119:166

A Borrowed Home

1919 - 1920

Selma with her youngest daughter, Ruth (approx. 1925)

After the foreclosure and loss of the homestead, Selma kept her children close. It was 1919 and she desperately felt the need to provide stability for her six children. This became her top priority. Over the past nine years the entire family had lived with death at the doorstep and uncertainty every day.

Selma decided to stay in her home. The new owner, Mohall State Bank, agreed to this and she was thankful. Time would allow her to sort things out and decide what was her next step. She was glad she wouldn't need to uproot her family so soon. This would give her time to think and decide what her next step in life would be.

Ruth was now the youngest. At the age of 13 she stayed at home with her mother when not in school. Ruth was her mother's constant companion. She was a happy child, but held fears untold from the loss of her father, brother, and home. Selma needed her presence as much as Ruth needed her mother.

Ester and Ingeborg were working for private families. Usually they lived with the family hiring them, but they were back and forth as they came home between jobs. These two girls were thorough and quick workers. They upheld the reputation of Swedish girls being outstanding domestic workers. Oftentimes during planting, harvesting, or after the birth of a new baby, a farm lady needed an extra pair of hands. Ester and Ingeborg were seldom together as they went from farm to farm. They cooked and cleaned for hired men and the family. They washed clothes and ironed. Their work started long before sunup and ended long after sundown.

During the harvest, young women were often hired to follow the threshing crew. They were usually assigned to the cook car. Here they slaved over a hot stove while making three huge meals a day for all of the men. It was hard work, but the pay was better than what a private home could offer. Sometimes the girls were gone for weeks as they moved from farm to farm while the crops were harvested.

Selma prayed that God would keep her precious girls safe. There were so many "drifters" hired and she feared that any one of these men could bring harm to a young woman. Together she discussed various ways that the girls could protect themselves and keep safe in these uncertain times. "Do whatever it takes to be safe," she warned.

Ester and Ingeborg (approx. 1915–1919)

The boys were working as general farm laborers. Their day started early and ended late just like their sisters'. It was dirty and hard backbreaking labor. It presented a different set of physical dangers, however, with horses, threshing machines, belts, and steam engines. One slip and injury or death could result.

Whenever possible the children came home to visit. It was always a joyful time when this happened. A house full of children graced Selma's heart with abundant blessings. She was so thankful for each and every one of them.

There was no way for Selma to keep her children tied to her. They were young with a youthful zest for life. Each one possessed their own set of dreams and ambitions for what lay ahead. They were less cautious than their mother and were positive and optimistic. In spite of all the family disasters,

John and Herman
(approx. 1916)

this next generation offered her hope. Hope for the future.

With the turn of a new year, Selma knew that she needed to move. It was 1920 and the economy showed little signs of turning around. Many people were under duress. There were more foreclosures and farm auctions than she had ever witnessed in all her days in America. Times were tough. Even the banks were beginning to falter.

If Selma was going to move it needed to be done quickly. Spring was just around the corner, and she had made the decision this would offer the best time for relocating to a new home. She bowed her head, "Please, God, give me direction. What do you want me to do? Where do you want me to go? If you lead, I will follow." ⬭

Erik (in the 1920s or later)

MAJOR
CHANGES

McKinney Bridge picture taken from the flour mill

"The LORD is good, a refuge in times of trouble. He cares for those who trust in Him."

Nahum 1:7

Reflections

1920s

The 1920s were not the most generous years for Dakota farmers. The clouds held little if any moisture and the ground was dry and parched. The grain grew and then wilted before the kernels could form and head out. The economic situation was beginning to take a nose-dive. Times were uncertain.

On November 29, 1918, Wm. Morse wrote in the *Grover News* for the *Tolley Journal*: "...the scribe has been up against it. Hasn't had a crop in three years and then he was turned down by a thresher who was supposed to thresh it, but pulled by and left without any just case [cause] or provocation." Later, others told in the same newspaper of their meager crops in Renville County.

Even if farmers had a fair crop, it was difficult to sell the grain. Elevators were not buying because the railroads were charging double and triple the amounts to ship it. This would result in a loss for the elevator.

A common saying was heard, "We buy retail and turn around and sell wholesale. There's no profit margin in farming if a person has to do this."

The Sjöqvist household was deeply in debt. There was little money to draw upon. Outstanding bills loomed.

Selma Sjoqvist internally struggled. "What should I do? I don't want to leave." But. Her children were off on their own adventures. They were at a job for two to eight weeks and then they would bounce back home for a time.

She couldn't expect them to walk in the financial mire which bogged her down. Selma was a gutsy and determined lady. She refused to ask for help.

As Selma walked across her former land, she pondered, prayed, and challenged herself. She attempted to rationalize what would be the best decision to make. Although the children offered emotional help now and then, Selma felt alone in her futile attempts to keep going. She knew there was only one thing to do as a result. She needed to leave. Oh, she still had dreams and hope. Just not here. Not in this, their first home. Selma had fought a good fight for about a decade. Johan would have been proud.

She entered her house and knew with certainty that this decision was not made lightly or quickly. The homesteading land where the family still resided held so many memories. The house she was about to leave had been built by her husband's hands and as the family had grown, he expanded it to meet their needs.

Selma thought, prayed, talked to friends and neighbors, and at last settled her sights on the village to the south. McKinney was a settlement nestled along the banks of the Mouse River about five miles as the crow flies.

In a new location there were abundant opportunities for the older children to find jobs. The McKinney Flour Mill was in operation, and the large Swenson families were constantly in need of help. With other farms in such close proximity the children would be able to come home more easily. Her children wouldn't have far to go to earn their wages.

As Selma's thoughts turned to moving, she stopped to look around her home. She couldn't help but reflect back. Selma had watched all five of her Dakota children grow as they labored side by side on the Grover township farmland. As a mother, she was humbled by their resilient and persistent labors as they desperately attempted to save the homestead.

In her hands, she held an empty crate as she started gathering her belongings. The boys would help her move everything once she was ready.

Holding the empty container in her hand, she looked around the house. The kitchen was always warm and alluring. Here she baked bread and prepared countless meals. The kitchen table was the place she wrote letters and the children played games.

In the living room Johan's shoemaking tools still lay idle on the small corner cabinet. Many shoes had lovingly been brought to life for the children.

In front of the window sat her spinning wheel. She loved to create the

MAP OF McKINNEY TOWNSHIP

Scale 1¾ inches to 1 mile

Township 161 North, Range 86 West of the 5th P. M.

The Standard Atlas of Renville County North Dakota, page 31; Geo. A. Ogle & Co., 1914.

yarn needed to knit mittens and socks for the cold Dakota days. This was another way she provided for her family.

As Selma walked, she bent down and picked up a toy that laid half hidden. She caressed the little teddy bear that Edwin had loved so dearly. She smiled as she thought of his scrungy, little toy. It was missing one ear, both eyes, and most of its fur. None of this had mattered to her little fellow. She brought it close and smelled. She thought she detected faint smells of Edwin, but than again maybe it was just a musty odor.

When Selma came to her bedroom, she looked at it with new eyes. This was the exact spot that she and Johan talked late into the evening as they felt so close to each other.

Leaving quickly before the tears would flow, Selma laughed when she came back full circle to the front door. Looking at it, she couldn't help but think about the day her dear daughter and son had walked through the door after their long journey from Sweden.

"Yes," she thought, "this house has had its share of sadness, but it has had even more love and laughter. Life has been good here."

In spite of the many setbacks, she remembered Johan had believed in this country and the golden opportunities before them. Their children would have countless chances offered to them that could never be realized in Sweden. The Dakota land may not have rendered gold. It may never

The second McKinney Mill (shown here) remained open until 1934. The first flour mill, built by Will J. Paff in 1903, burned in 1906.

make them rich, but they had freedoms untold. Her children could own their own homes, property, and possessions. Job opportunities promised steady income. Johan had often reminded her that it was all worth the sacrifices they would need to make. God would never leave them or forsake them. No matter what.

And so, Selma completed packing. She took one last look around the little house that had been her home. Slowly, she picked up the last container.

Selma reluctantly lost the only land she and her husband had ever owned. And now the loss was compounded by leaving this house that had been their home. Once again Selma needed to turn from her hurt and refocus. She would create new visions and goals. McKinney would be the perfect spot for her to continue to nurture her family. Here she would have the support of many other Swedish friends. Some of these families had lived in the little settlement for years and were well established.

Before opening the door to depart, she bowed her head. "Thank you God for all the years granted to me in this home. I pray that you will bless me and my family in this new venture."

As she closed the door, Selma surveyed the homestead land for the last time. She looked down at the pile of belongings stacked in front of her. Now, she was ready.

   ℘   LONG BEFORE SHE COULD SEE the car approaching, she heard it rumble along the trail. John bounced along in his older, used and somewhat banged-up Ford car. He had been so proud when he made the purchase. His brother, Herman, sat beside him. John stopped the vehicle close to the front door and the young fellows jumped down from the front seat. After greeting their mother, they loaded her boxes and a few pieces of furniture.

Before starting the car again, the two young men glanced over at Selma with concerned looks. "Are you ready, Mor?"

Then they looked at each other when they heard her determined voice. "Ja. You bet! McKinney, here I come."

John put the car in gear and slowly pulled away from the Sjöqvist homestead. ∞

"But I trust in your unfailing love; my heart rejoices in your salvation. I will sing to the LORD, for He has been good to me."
Psalm 13:5-6

Giving Up and Letting Go

1920

Selma moved in the spring of 1920 and quickly came to love her new home in McKinney. It was closer to many of her Swedish-speaking friends. She could easily walk a few yards and have coffee with someone nearby. The children were closer to their work, which offered them many more visits home. She loved this aspect the most. Everyone and everything appeared to settle in quickly.

Living in McKinney, Selma had many of the same amenities. The same Mouse River flowed south through the settlement. The fish were there for the catching. She knew in time she'd locate the berry patches. She just needed to venture out to find them.

There was one aspect of her new location that eased her greatest burden. She was in close proximity to the McKinney Cemetery. She frequently

McKinney in the early 1900s

visited Johan and little Edwin's graves. She would sit and talk to Johan. Here Selma shed tears. At times she even came to laugh as she shared tidbits with her departed spouse.

Summer turned to fall. Harvest was once again in full swing. Everyone was on the run. Her children were working with the area threshing crews. The farms they worked on were awaiting the arrival of the yearly rig and the fast and rugged pace of bringing in the crop.

This year the homestead house would have a totally different use. The new owners of her old home would be using it as a granary. She had mixed

McKINNEY

McKINNEY TWP.   Scale: 300 ft = 1 inch

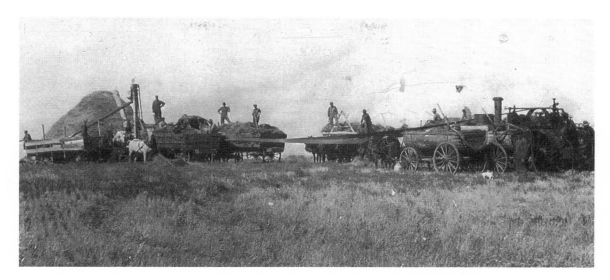

emotions about all this. It was difficult to grasp her home being filled with something other than people and love. On the other hand, it wouldn't be housing strangers. At times, in some strange way, it even appeared appropriate.

A typical threshing crew of the local area. The Sjöqvist children worked on this one.

On Thursday, October 6, 1920 the threshing crew finished harvesting the 160-acre former Sjöqvist homestead. The house had just been filled with 250 bushels of grain. The threshing rig pulled away from the farmstead and headed off for the next place of harvest.

The crew was nearly at their next destination when someone looked back. They saw big, black billowing smoke rising from the hills they had just left. What was going on?

A few of the men rode off on horses. They were heading back to check on what could possibly be creating such a large amount of smoke. What in the world could be on fire?

When they arrived back at the Sjöqvist homestead, the entire house/granary was engulfed in flames. There was absolutely no way to save either the house or harvest. It would be a total loss.

Was it started by a spark from the big tractor or threshing rig? Was the grain too damp to be stored without drying properly? So many things could have resulted in combustion. Once it had a spark, there was no possible way to stop it.

> Fire destroyed the home on the Sjoquist homestead up the river north of town Thursday afternoon, the fire starting immediately after the threshing rig had left the place. The house was used for storing grain and contained about 250 bushels that had just been threshed, and the house and grain are a complete loss.

The *Renville County Farmers Press* (October 7, 1920)

Selma thought about her former home even more in the next few weeks. It was sad to have her house lost in such a tragic way. Maybe, just maybe, God was helping her put the personal loss of her homestead to rest.

"God works in mysterious ways. It is my job to trust," she reminded herself daily. ∽

Note: The land had been sold on December 10, 1919 to W. W. Bergman and his wife, Laura. This couple had purchased it from the Mohall State Bank for a mere one dollar plus costs. The Assistant Cashier of the Mohall State Bank signed his name as A. R. Bergman. For reasons unknown, W. W. Bergman and wife, Laura, turned it back to the Mohall State Bank.

With the loss of the 250 bushels of grain on October 6, 1920 and many other factors, a sheriff's deed forced the Mohall State Bank to relinquish the Sjöqvist homestead on August 20, 1925. The State Bank of Commerce of Minneapolis purchased it for $2,281.59.

By the year 1944 it had been sold a number of times over and was owned by Norman Knutson, Joseph Knutson's son. Joseph as a young man had assisted Johan in building the homestead shack. Today the west half is owned by Judith Knutson (another relative) and the east half is owned by Lyle Alexander. Lyle's son Jon, formerly from Tolley, is married to Cindy Hellebust from Grover. They now farm this half of the homestead.

The Swenson log cabin, built around 1886, was moved from the old buffalo crossing to the northwest corner of the McKinney Cemetery and restored in 1937 by the Department of the Interior.

"And we know that in all things God works for the good of those who love him, who have been called according to his purpose."

Romans 8:28

A Refuge

1921 – 1936

Life settled down somewhat for Selma and her remaining family. McKinney was a beautiful location with rich soil and the slow, meandering Mouse River. Selma missed the farm, but she was so thankful for the place she had found to live. McKinney was an up-and-coming small settlement of about 200. Many people and businesses had moved into the area. The community thrived with the busy flour mill, bakery, lumberyard, hardware store, bank, butcher shop, newspaper office, Bertleson Trading Company, and much more.

Selma's children were also doing well. Since they were all good workers, they easily found employment on the large farms surrounding the area. Some were at the large Swenson farms. Nels, Frank, Edward, and John Swenson were a few that offered jobs. These families were good to the Sjöqvist family. In return the farmers received respect and good hard labor.

Times were changing. When the railroad failed to come to McKinney, some of the businesses and a number of people left for the village of Tolley, west and south of Selma's home, less than five miles away.

Even though some of her friends had left, most had stayed. Life was still good. Selma's older children were marrying and slowly leaving the nest. Erik and Ruth, now her two youngest, stayed with her the longest. They had a loyalty to their Mor and were fierce protectors.

The Sjöqvist family continued to be a close-knit group. They gathered for holidays and stopped in frequently for visits.

ℴ   ONE CHRISTMAS WHEN the young couples came home to Selma, there was much excitement. The married children now had children of their own. There was joy and merriment as they gathered together with all the little ones.

The young families struggled financially to make ends meet. Purchasing gifts cost money and the grandchildren knew they shouldn't request anything from their elders.

So, it was truly a wonderful surprise for the older grandchildren to each receive a bag with a pencil and a big red tablet with a picture of an Indian chief on the front. Wow! This was really unexpected. Later they learned that all the adults had pooled their money together to buy these special, precious gifts.

ℴ   TIME PASSED AND in 1934 rumors ran wild. The talk was that the government was coming in and taking over their land. Could this happen? Not in America. The community was in disbelief. This was the very reason many had left the Old Country.

Anger set in when rumor became reality. In 1935 the US Government purchased 22,000 acres along the Mouse River. It included everything in the valley from two miles north of the Mouse River Park, south to the Renville County line, and into Ward County. It would be turned into the Upper Souris Wildlife Game Refuge and Preserve.

Plans were underway by the government to totally change the landscape forever. A large dam would be built at the county line to the south to hold back the waters of the Mouse (Souris) River and create Lake Darling. Lake Darling got its name from the political cartoonist Jay N. "Ding" Darling. He became director of the newly formed Bureau of Biological Survey. The duck population had diminished during the dry years of the 1930s and Darling pushed the Duck Stamp Act through Congress. Proceeds from the sale of the stamps were used to purchase land for the Upper Souris National Wildlife Refuge.

And so, the government brought in crews. They cut every tree that grew below the flood water line. This meant all trees were downed in low places from the north end of the refuge area to one mile north of the village of Greene. Trees were later used for snow fences, bird shelters, or burned.

Additional plans included using the lumber salvaged from homes and businesses doomed by water for construction of buildings at the CCC camps

(Civilian Conservation Corp) at Mohall, Kenmare, and places throughout North Dakota and Montana.

The beautiful, scenic trail that ran along the west side of the river was now fenced off from public use. Gorgeous scenery was lost to all future generations. Instead, people viewed an immense body of water with multiple "No Trespassing" signs. Fishing was now allowed only in a few places. Planned government flooding destroyed farms and homes for 32 miles down the valley.

McKinney, looking from the direction where the flour mill stood (2009)

The loss of revenue and population for the area was daunting. People received a small compensation for their homes and businesses before being forced to move. The amount of money received from the US government was pennies on the dollar. Tax money received from the area dropped considerably. Residents moved hither-thither and yon. Some moved to Tolley while many others left for far-off points in North Dakota and states beyond.

These were hard times for our nation. The depression had hit with a vengeance. Now displaced people had to find new work, when jobs were already extremely scarce. They needed new homes wherever they could find them. For some their whole identity was lost forever. These were homesteaders who came to the area leaving everything and everyone they loved behind. They had crossed a wide ocean with determination for a better way of life. They couldn't understand what was happening to them. After giving up all they had in one country, fighting and working hard in another, now it was all being taken from them. Why?

For over fifty years some of the people had tilled the soil. All the years of blood, sweat, and tears put into the soil were all for naught. These homesteaders could not fight and win against the US government. It was truly a sad day when the government forced all the people to leave their beautiful valley. Farmers, business owners, home dwellers, and the entire town of McKinney left.

As Selma sat with her family around her, she watched her home destroyed. The government promise of the lumber being used for CCC camps had given comfort knowing Selma's home would live on in some remote capacity. Instead, the government officials had lied. She witnessed a big bulldozer come into the McKinney village. And then the unthinkable. The noisy, smoky machine rolled up to Selma's home. With a mighty thrust it pushed her beautiful home to the ground. To compound the grief everyone watched as it was burned.

She was joined by other valley dwellers on a hill above McKinney. Tears flowed freely. Everyone felt loss and sadness for the destruction of a beautiful valley, a meandering river, and the camaraderie of longtime friends. The community was demolished and McKinney was lost forever. Left in its place was a distrust for the US government.

Wiping the tears from her cheeks, Selma lifted her chin. Once again she felt the need to lead her adult family. Gathering them close to her, she thanked God for each of them. She prayed for God's love, guidance, and support.

Picking up her few belongings she struck out on yet another adventure. She was leaving with Ruth and Erik for the Jamestown, North Dakota area. Here she would live near the towns of Ypsilanti and Montpelier.

Life would go on. With God's help she would begin another adventure. ∽

Note: Today all that remains of McKinney is the cemetery and the McKinney bridge that crosses the Mouse River.
Photo: Dawn Christianson (2006)

Selma Sjöqvist's family before leaving McKinney, most likely the fall of 1936. All family members are present except John who was probably taking the picture.

Selma's Children and Grandchildren
Ester and Claus with Edwin
Herman and Myrtle with Dolly & Duane; mother-in-law, Lilly (Mrs. Jessie) Shortridge
John and Bernice with Marie, Eunice, Norman, Gordon, and Mae
Ingeborg and Ray with June, Justin, Dale, Glee, and Jerry
Erik (not yet married)
Ruth (not yet married)

McKinney after the 1904 flood waters had receded several feet

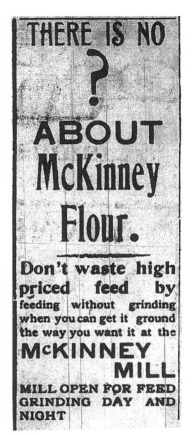

The second McKinney bridge

Ad in *The Tolley Journal*,
September 3, 1909

Ad in the *Mouse River Journal*,
March 3, 1905

The first McKinney Mill – built by Jacob Paff – started milling flour
on November 5, 1903. It was destroyed by fire. The mill dam (spillway
shown on right) also furnished power for a six-boat Merry-Go-Round.

MAGNET TO
THE WEST

"May the LORD keep watch between you and me when we are away from each other."

Genesis 31:49

Moving West

mid-1940s

Erik was the first of the Sjöqvist family to move to California. As he drove the long road to the West Coast, Erik desperately hoped he was doing the right thing. All news reports of jobs being easily accessible had pointed him in this direction, but he hated the idea of leaving family behind in North Dakota. In some ways he thought he had left behind two mothers, Ester who had cared for him for many years and his real Mor, Selma.

Like his father, Johan, he also desired and dreamed of the riches offered in the West. And like his predecessor, Erik knew there could be no turning back. In a way he was the pioneer now as he checked out the lure of jobs in a faraway state. In doing this, he realized he was more like the father he had never known. He was filled with excitement. And so, he whistled as he drove down the never-ending trail.

After arriving in California, the first thing Erik did was to find a place to stay. Then he went out job hunting. He was quickly hired at the Pacific Coast shipyards. It was backbreaking, hard labor, but it provided the necessary money he needed for a start.

It didn't take Erik long to realize the work in the shipyards would only be temporary. It could never be his lifelong career. However, the very thing he left behind in North Dakota was also the very thing he now desperately wanted as his occupation. He knew he could be successful here as a blacksmith. Finding an empty garage, he started advertising his business. In his repair shop he welded and did blacksmithing for others. His work was steady in this post-war era. Everyone needed help with something. Because money wasn't flush, people were making do with what they had and so vehicles and other equipment were repaired rather than replaced.

Erik wrote home often. He told everyone back in Dakota about this warm and wonderful state. "California is a place where the sun shines every single day." He related little tidbits about his blacksmithing business. He was anxious for his loved ones to know he was fine and doing well.

Selma was elated to hear of Erik's newfound success. While she was happy for him, she missed her now youngest son with the fierce love of a mother. She had longed for Erik and Ester for the ten years they had been separated with an ocean between them. When the family had been reunited, she had made a vow to never let such a distance ever keep them so far apart. But, once again she was removed from the closeness of her son, this time by an ocean of earth.

Selma lived with her daughter Ruth and husband Virgil. Inside, Selma was torn. She loved living with Ruth and being close to Ester in Ypsilanti, North Dakota, but she ached for Erik and wanted to be close to him also. Thousands of miles separated her and Ester from Erik.

Everything was once again in emotional turmoil for Selma. Why was the West always pulling loved ones apart? Was there a giant magnet attracting movement farther and farther west? First it was America and now the state of California. What next? ∞

Erik with his car

"And now,...fear the LORD your God, to walk in all his ways, to love him, to serve the LORD your God with all your heart and with all your soul, and to observe the LORD's commands and decrees that I am giving you today for your own good."

Deuteronomy 10:12

The Second Move

mid to late-1940s

S elma took comfort in having her first grandson Edwin nearby. Ester and Claus lived near her in Ypsilanti, North Dakota, only a few miles down the road. Edwin was Ester and Claus's only child. He was special to his Mormor because he bore the name of Selma's youngest child, who now lay near his Far beneath the earth in the McKinney Cemetery.

But most children grow up. And Selma's grandson, Edwin Johan Johnson, did just that.

As an adult he had some untold ailments. He searched for medical answers far and wide and ended up in California. After going to a doctor there, he found some relief.

Upon returning to North Dakota Edwin married a North Dakota gal from Nortonville. Her name was Edna Marie Podoll. Their wedding was held ten weeks after Ruth and Virgil's in the exact same church.

Edna was a trained nurse and encouraged her new husband to relocate closer to better medical assistance. Edna also yearned to embark on far-off adventures and encouraged a move to the West. At last Edwin gathered enough courage and with his wife, Edna, left North Dakota. He ventured west to California, following in his uncle Erik's footsteps.

Erik had begun an exodus that Edwin and Edna were now continuing. The Sjöqvist family migration had been started when Johan had left the land he knew to search out better opportunities for his family, and now the following generations were doing the same. Jobs and an enticing future were pulling family continually westward. From all the way across the Atlantic ocean... over the vast expanse of America... and on to another ocean. The gigantic Pacific. ∞

Edwin and Edna Johnson's wedding, July 14, 1946

Neighbor girl, Raymond and Lela Atwood (Ingeborg's children) at Edwin and Edna's wedding, July 1946

"Be strong and courageous. Do not be terrified; do not be discouraged, for the Lord your God will be with you wherever you go."

Joshua 1:9

What Should She Do?

late 1940s

At the time of Erik and Edwin's moves, Selma was still living with Ruth and her husband Virgil in Ypsilanti, North Dakota. Virgil worked on various farms in the area, but had no real interest in farming himself. Upon hearing from Erik and later Edwin of the abundant opportunities available in the West, both Ruth and Virgil felt the tug of this up-and-coming state.

When Ruth and Virgil presented their thoughts to Selma, she felt trapped. On one hand if she moved, she would be closer to two of her children, Erik and Ruth, and her grandson, Edwin. On the other hand if Selma left North Dakota she would be leaving her daughter Ester and husband Claus, along with three other married children.

What should she do? She pleaded with God to speak to her.

Selma knew if she decided to stay in North Dakota, she could request to live with Ester. But what would that say to Ruth? Would this offend the daughter who had stuck with her mother through thick and thin? Ruth had never moved away from Selma even after she married Virgil.

Turning everything over to God, Selma prayed for an answer. She needed peace in whatever decision she made. Her children meant the world to her. She loved each and every one of them dearly.

In her deliberation Selma leaned toward venturing West with Ruth and Virgil. Along with Ester, she would be leaving behind Herman, John, and Ingeborg in the Kenmare/McKinney/Tolley area. These three seemed more settled in their lives. Herman was married and living in Kenmare. John was deeply entrenched in blacksmithing and raising a large family. Ingeborg was also married. She and her husband Raymond were farming and raising their family. All of them seemed satisfied and directed in their lives.

Finally Selma spoke to Ester. As a mother Selma poured her heart out to her oldest child. Ester sat quietly and listened.

Because Ester had been independent for most of her growing-up years, Selma and Ester looked at each other more as equals and less as mother and daughter. Ester knew how difficult it must be for her mother to be the one leaving. Again.

Selma's feelings were similar to what she had when embarking for America so many years ago. As a young mother in Sweden, her heart had broken as she waved good-bye to her oldest and youngest children, Ester and Erik. These two had stood and watched as she, their mother, had walked away.

Ester also had flashbacks of that long-ago experience. As an eight year old, she had watched her mother go, leaving her behind. She had felt abandoned and cried inconsolably. She had been left to help her mother's parents care for one-year-old baby Erik. This little boy had been her driving force to be strong and to put one foot in front of the other for ten long years.

Selma Sjoqvist (1946)

Ester held her mother in her arms. "Go Mother! Go with Ruth!"

"But, I don't want to leave you again!" Selma tried to be strong for Ester, but tears refused to stop as they coursed down her face.

"Mother, Claus and I have been discussing what it would be like for us to pack our bags and join up with Edwin and Edna. If we knew you would be there too, our decision would be so much easier. So, just go! We'll be there before you know it. Okay?"

Selma nodded her head and hugged her eldest child. What a rock this child was to her.

She knew in her heart that Ester had been a part of God's answer to prayers. He had just spoken to her through the words of her eldest child. "'Go in peace!' saith the Lord," Selma repeated over and over to herself.

Selma finally reached peace and made a firm commitment to leave North Dakota. "Ja, I vill go!" ∽

*"You turned my wailing into dancing;
you removed my sackcloth and clothed
me with joy, that my heart may sing to
you and not be silent. O LORD my God,
I will give you thanks forever."*

Psalm 30:11-12

Wrestling and Dancing

late 1940s – 1950s

Selma and Ruth
Olson

Selma had dreaded leaving North Dakota. She had labored over the decision. To leave or not to leave? Once everything was packed, she set her sights once again on a new beginning. She wondered what adventures would await her in California. Like times of old she felt an eagerness in her heart for what lay ahead. She was excited!

It was the post-war years of the late 1940s. World War II had ended. The dynamics of California were changing as a result of the war. Many women had become instant widows. Men returning from the war were unable to keep their homes. Funds were short and homes were put on the market, as families searched for cheaper housing.

There was no question that Selma, Ruth's mother, would be a viable part of Virgil and Ruth's household. With this in mind they searched for something that would suit their needs.

They all found exactly what they wanted in Lawndale, a suburb of Los Angeles. It was west of the large metropolitan area and closer to the ocean. The house was small, but affordable. It had two bedrooms, a kitchen, living room, an open-air front veranda, and covered back steps which served as the major family entrance into the home.

The backyard was sufficient. In time it would hold a number of clothes lines and a small garage with an alley out behind. A low cement barrier from the front of the property to the back served as a fence and separated their yard and the neighbor's yard to the left. Beautiful trees in the back offered some shade and yet allowed sufficient sun to shine through. For the first time ever they enjoyed their very own fresh lemons and oranges.

The Lawndale, California home of Virgil and Ruth Olson

An old shed held a few chickens and birds that Virgil cared for and loved dearly. There was no city ordinance against raising farm animals at the time, so families here and there in the neighborhood enjoyed animals in their backyards.

Virgil soon found steady employment with a construction crew. Supervisors eagerly hired anyone coming from the Dakotas. They felt people from this area had strong work ethics, were reliable and of good moral character.

Selma felt better in the dry California air. It seemed easier for her to breathe and she was less prone to illness. This brought peace and comfort to both her Dakota and California children.

It didn't take too many years before Virgil and Ruth purchased their first television. The three would sit and watch shows together. But, Selma loved to watch "her" shows. When watching one of her favorites, "Saturday Night Wrestling," her face would emanate the pain and torture of each headlock or body pin. She enjoyed the wrestlers Gorgeous George and Red Berry and would cheer for their victories. When Saturday night arrived, no one else in the house had a choice. Wrestling ruled!

Selma knew every wrestling rule and could have called the match from the edge of the ring. Television and radio audiences would have loved her deeply involved commentaries. She was absolutely amazing to watch as she glued her eyes to the small black and white television.

"American Bandstand" was another of her favorite television programs. Music was special to Selma. Oftentimes she would dance around in time to the music. She would once again be in the arms of her beloved Johan as

Selma Amanda
Dahlgren Sjöqvist
(1956)

she imagined the shear joy of the smooth rhythm and the nearness of her long-gone husband. In her mind it was real and her happiness was deep and profound.

One day Selma's dancing rendition ended when she collided with the coffee table. Her daydreams of "long ago" abruptly came to an end. She doubled-up on the floor of the living room with excruciating pain. Ruth and Virgil immediately called for help.

As Selma was being loaded into the ambulance, she looked at Ruth. "How will I explain this? No one will believe that it happened while I was dancing to 'American Bandstand' music." Then she gave a faint hint of a smile, "Well, at least it will give them something to laugh about."

Selma had broken her hip. After a stay in the hospital she was sent home to recuperate. In time it healed, but she never walked again. Even though she was limited in her physical movement, her mind remained active and alert.

She continued to watch her two most favorite television shows. Now, it was with a little less vigor. Her docile cat lay on her bed close to her.

Inside though, she still was wrestling and dancing. She verbalized the wrestling moves and sang along to the music of the dance band. She was alive and well. ∞

LIVES OF
CHILDREN

Esther Johnson

~~Herman J. Sjöqvist~~

John Ragnar Julius Sjöqvist

Ingeborg Atwood

Erik Knut Valdemar Sjöqvist

Ruth Josefin Helena Sjöqvist

Edwin Sigmund Herbert Sjöqvist

Selma Amanda Sjöqvist

John A. Sjöqvist

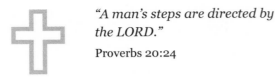

"A man's steps are directed by the LORD."

Proverbs 20:24

A Visitor From the North

1913 – 1921

Ester Sjöqvist first met Mr. Claus Johnson in the fall of 1920. She was working for various farmers in the McKinney area and had been in the United States for the past five years. She loved being close to her family, especially her mother, Selma. She had grown up for ten years away from her Mor. Although she missed her native country, McKinney had become her home.

Ester had good command of the English language and adapted quickly to the new ways of Dakota. She was nearly 24 years old when she met Mr. Johnson. Her next birthday was just around the corner on December first.

ᗍ⟩   IN 1913 BEING A FARMER in Sweden was extremely difficult and nearly impossible. Land ownership was next to nil. The small farms were passed on to the oldest son or sometimes divided up amongst the total number of sons. When division of land was the choice of the departed parents, the small portion left to each person made it very difficult to eke out a living.

As a result young men who yearned for farms and tilling the soil felt a calling and a real lust to embark on journeys to the New World. Land was available and each year more land was opened up in the West. This was true both in the United States and also in Canada.

Shortly after Klas Henrikson celebrated his 21st birthday, he made the decision to leave his homeland. Indeed he had doubts and fears of what lay ahead of him, but the lure of land and adventure pulled even stronger.

Klas, born June 5, 1892, was the son of Henrik Johansson and Anna Andersdotter. He was their third living son with older brothers, Johan and Ivar. Three other children had died between these two brothers and his birth. He also had a sister, Anna, who was two years younger. The family lived in Istorp, southeast of Göteborg in Västergötland, Sweden.

Klas Henrikson
Johnson (1921)

Klas had received letters from others, including his brother, who had gone before him. They related to Klas that Canada offered abundant, good farm land. All he needed was to be brave enough to come and snatch up these opportunities before they were all gone.

Klas boarded the *Scandinavian* at the docks in Glasgow, Scotland. He doubted that he would ever set foot on his native soil again. With renewed determination he stepped on deck even while realizing there was absolutely no turning back.

Once the *Scandinavian* set sail and left the harbor, Klas began to focus his thoughts to what lay before him. There was no sense dwelling in the past. He had a whole lifetime in front of him. He was eager and ready.

Sailing on the high seas in 1913 was not an easy feat. People became sick and a few even died. Klas was young and strong. He faired well in his crossing. He spent much of his time visiting with others who were making the journey. Together they swapped stories of bygone days and made plans for what Canada would offer them as immigrants.

The days passed quickly and on the eighth of July in 1913 the vessel pulled into the harbor of Quebec. Klas had $25 cash in his pocket. He needed to declare this amount to authorities and also lay out his plans before entering. Having enough money would prove to immigration officials that he could be self-sufficient.

Klas was relieved to know that he had thought things through before disembarking. His brother was already farming. And so, he told authorities that he was headed to Saskatoon, Saskatchewan. They asked how he planned to get there and his rapid reply was by Canadian Pacific Railway. He also reiterated that he had every intention of farming once he arrived at his destination.

Klas wasn't quite clear how or where he'd end up once he arrived in

Saskatoon, but he definitely knew he'd be farming either in Saskatchewan or Alberta.

As a young man Klas Henrikson had many unanswered questions, but the one thing he did know was his strong desire to become more acclimated to his new country. He decided then and there to start by changing his name. Because it was customary in Sweden for a young man to add "son" to the father's first name, Klas had used the name "Henrikson." However, from this point on he'd be known as Claus Johnson. That name sounded good and fit him well.

Time passed and Claus did find that his new country treated him well. He loved farming and working in the dirt.

For years he worked for other people. In 1916 Claus resided in Battle River, Alberta. And from there he moved on to Hardisty, Alberta. Moving around was quite common for newcomers to a new country. Everyone was desperately working hard to figure out how and also where they could and would fit in. At last he settled in Hughenden. He liked the small rural community and the rich black soil.

Claus knew he had made the right decision to come to a new country so far removed from Sweden, his homeland. He had countless opportunities in Canada and was eager for each and every one of them.

 ℂ JOHNSON HAD HEARD a lot about the McKinney area from a friend who had once lived there. Carl Swenson now lived in Owen, Alberta. He often made trips back to McKinney to visit his parents, Mr. and Mrs. N. P. Swenson. The Swensons lived on prime land in the McKinney valley. During Carl's visits south, Claus would often accompany him to North Dakota.

The *Renville County Farmers Press,* under McKinney Mumbles, February 10, 1921

> Claude Johnson has returned to his home in Canada, he has been spending the winter so far with H. Sjoqvist and stated before he left that McKinney was the only place to live.

It was on one of these visits with Carl that Claus decided to stay for the winter. Although he had visited the area before, this time he planned to find a place to live for a few months.

Arriving in McKinney after the crops were off in Alberta, Claus Johnson searched for a place. Someone had pointed out Herman Sjöqvist as a possible answer for temporary residency.

And so it was that Herman took on a boarder for the winter. Herman and Claus did many things together and became fast friends.

During this time Ester visited not only her mother, but also her brothers and sisters. After ten years of separation, she yearned to build a closer relationship with her family.

On one of Ester's visits to see her brother Herman she officially met Mr. Johnson. Ester had seen him previously, but couldn't quite remember his first name. Was it Claus or was it Claude?

It was both. Officially, Johnson was known as Claude, but most of his friends called him Claus. Ester thought the name Claude was too confusing and stuck to the easy-to-say-name of Claus.

Throughout that winter Ester got to know this blond, blue-eyed young Swede from the North country she called Claus. He was not overly tall at five feet nine inches, but he was captivating. He was soft spoken and kind to everyone he met. Ester was enamored with him. Over the months Ester and Claus became known as a couple throughout the McKinney community.

When it came time for Claus to return to Alberta in February of 1921, he had come to love the people and land of this Dakota area. He often said, "McKinney is the only place to live."

But more than the land and acquaintances would be missed. He could hardly bare to leave Ester. He definitely knew that he had come to deeply care and love her.

Ester felt the same way. They had even discussed marriage.

Ester knew her heart lay with the Swede in Canada. And so, less than three months after Claus's departure, she boarded the Canadian Pacific Railroad and headed to Alberta and her future husband, Claus.

On May 7, 1921 Ester became Mrs. Claude Johnson. Or was it Mrs. Claus Johnson? It really didn't matter. She was thrilled to become Mrs. Johnson as they tied the knot in Hardisty, Alberta, Canada.

Wedding picture of Claus and Ester Johnson, May 7, 1921

"Be completely humble and gentle; be patient, bearing with one another in love."

Ephesians 4:2

Homesick

1921 – 1922

In the spring of 1921, Claus worked on the farm like he'd done for the past eight years. He felt at home in Canada and on the farm in Hughenden, Alberta. It was extra special this year. Now, he was living with his new and lovely bride, Ester.

Ester Sjöqvist Johnson also loved being married and living with her husband, however, she knew no one else in the area. At times she felt so lonely. She was once again a foreigner in a foreign country. This was her third country of residency in six years.

Ester washed, cleaned, and scrubbed every square inch of their home. Nothing was left untouched as she worked to fill an inner void.

When Claus was home with her, things were great. But, the long days drug out for Ester as she waited in eager anticipation each evening for Claus's return from the farm fields. Each day Ester became more homesick.

All this took a change when she found out that she was carrying a child. Claus's baby was growing within her. The loneliness was somewhat curbed and replaced with pure joy and excited anticipation. A new generation was about to be born. Knitting and sewing tiny clothing added to her days.

Even though Ester never complained to her husband about her abrupt loss of family, Claus sensed that something was not quite right with his wife. "Yes, we are both overjoyed with the expectant arrival of our new baby, but what in the world is wrong with Ester? She's just not acting the way I know her."

Day after day an unspoken wall of questions arose between them. Ester just couldn't bring herself to explain her feelings to Claus. "He'll just think I'm complaining. I'll have to learn to live here. But why, oh Lord, does my family need to live so very far away from me? I miss my little brother, Erik, and my Mor."

Claus on the other hand, reasoned that it must be the new baby that was upsetting Ester. "But, she seems so excited about the baby." He continued to ponder and worry.

One day he came home to find Ester in tears. "What is the matter?" he asked. "Did you hurt yourself? Is it the baby? Did I do something wrong?"

Ester couldn't hold it in any longer. "Oh, Claus, I'm so sorry! I just miss my family in McKinney so much. I can hardly bear it. It's not you or the baby, but I've just missed out on so many years without my Mor, brothers, and sisters. And now, I'm gone again."

Claus took Ester in his arms. "Is that all it is?" he said, with a sigh of relief. "We can fix that. I've always wanted to live in McKinney. We'll just go there. We can have our baby in North Dakota and live happily ever after. Now, dry your tears and we'll make plans. Okay?"

And so it was that Claus and Ester boarded the Canadian Pacific Railroad and headed south for McKinney, North Dakota. It was December 17, 1921 when they entered the United States by crossing the border at Portal, North Dakota.

Ester, Edwin and Claus (about 1929)

The two arrived in time to spend Christmas with the entire Sjöqvist family at Mor's home. No one was happier than Ester. She continually thanked her thoughtful and loving husband for all that he gave up for her happiness. His act of kindness endeared him to her even more than before.

Approximately seven weeks after their arrival in McKinney, Claus and Ester Johnson became the proud parents of a baby boy. He was born on February 4, 1922. They named him Edwin Johan Johnson. His first name was the same as Ester's seven-year-old brother who had died shortly after her arrival in America. Johan had been her father's name who had passed away in 1911, just a few years before her arrival to America. It was also Claus' brother's name and Ester's Morfar.

Ester and Claus's little Edwin would be the first grandson born into the Sjöqvist family. Everyone was thrilled.

As Ester and Claus admired their little fellow, they were so thankful God had blessed them with a heavenly bundle of joy. They were equally thrilled to be living close to so many loved ones in the beautiful McKinney River Valley. God was indeed good! ❧

Claus (late 1940s)

Four generations: Ester, Selma, Sherry, Edwin (1949 or 1950)

*"Listen, my sons, to a father's instruction;
pay attention and gain understanding.
I give you sound learning, so do not
forsake my teaching."*

Proverbs 4:1-2

The Oldest Son

1896 – 1960

Selma and Johan had been thrilled when Herman Gunnar Emanuel Sjöqvist was born on November 14, 1896. It was exciting to have a son. Little Herman grew quickly and made every attempt to mimic the actions of his tall and upright father.

At the age of six Herman wandered around the house searching for his Far. Over and over Selma explained that Far had sailed away to America. He had no idea where "America" was. During the time of his father's absence, Herman yearned for a dominant male figure. He found this in his maternal grandfather, Johan Dahlgren. He stuck close to his side, wherever he went. His appreciation of Morfar's presence was extra special because he was Herman's only grandfather. In his Far's family down the road only Farmor and an aunt were living.

It was a very happy day a year and a half later when Herman's mother, Selma, informed him that he, along with his brother, John, and sister, Ingeborg, would soon leave for America. Herman would be able to be with his dear father once again.

His happiness was replaced on the day of departure with fear. It was pretty scary for a wide-eyed youngster of seven to leave the comfort of his Swedish grandfather. He waved good-bye to his big sister, Ester, and hugged his baby brother, Erik. These two were held in the arms of his grandfather and grandmother. His mother, brother, and sister departed with him. They were off for America.

After arriving in North Dakota, the new American homestead was pretty bare. In many ways it reminded Herman of Sweden. Herman was a big help on the farm. His father came to respect his young son's strengths and abilities. Together with his younger brother, John, the trio tilled the soil and cared for the animals. Throughout each and every task Herman paid close attention to every move his father made.

Herman was deeply concerned when his father became ill in May of 1910. But his worry paled in comparison to what he felt in October of 1911. On the third of the month the family sat beside Johan Alfred Sjöqvist's bedside and said their final farewells.

Herman didn't know what to feel. He was now the "oldest man" in the family, yet he wasn't even fifteen. The last thing in the world he wanted was total responsibility of his mother, brothers, and sisters. He ached inside. He knew that his childhood was over and he was now thrust into an adult world. He felt total devastation. All the carefree days with the hopes and dreams he anticipated in North Dakota would soon be buried in the McKinney Cemetery.

Herman, approximately 11 years old (1907)

ᔕ FIVE MONTHS AFTER his father's death, on March 31, 1912, Herman nervously walked down the church aisle with his brother John. It was confirmation day for his class of fifteen. They had been instructed in their native tongue of Swedish. He was proud to stand beside John in the Evangelical Lutheran Church in Tolley. Every pew was filled with family and friends. His Mor, brother, and sisters sat together. The place in the pew where his Far usually sat was empty. If only his dad were alive to witness his special day.

ᔕ HERMAN WRESTLED WITH his deep concerns for family. Both the ones in America and also those left in Sweden.

There was no dodging the heavy responsibility that hung across Herman's shoulders. He could deny it, try to avoid it, attempt to get out of it, but in the end he had to face it.

Herman needed to find a paying job. Sitting idle would never help purchase food. He needed to eat. And he must add to the fund for bringing his brother and sister from Sweden. It would take many pooled resources.

Herman did find odd jobs with farmers up and down the valley. Nothing was very substantial for a young man of fifteen. But, he knew every little bit would add to the family coffers.

At times he would persuade John to join him in the exploits of young men. It didn't take long for some of the less scrupulous men of the neighborhood to pick out easy prey. These men would entice the two in the folly of card playing and alcohol. The same fellows always seemed to know when payday rolled around.

Herman's sense of responsibility lightened somewhat in 1915. Ester and Erik made it to North Dakota. Now he could have that account settled and taken care of. But, the lightness of the load became heavier again with the death of little brother, Edwin. Would the tightness in his chest ever go away?

&ɔ ONCE HERMAN SIGNED his military registration card, it didn't take long for him to be drafted. He left for Camp Lewis, Washington on August 28, 1918. World War I was winding down and ended on November 11, 1918. Herman was discharged on January 25, 1919 after five months of service.

Returning home at the age of 22, he lived for a time with his mother, Selma, in Grover Township. Eventually he found a place in McKinney which was closer to places of work.

During the winter of 1920 and 1921, a man from Canada inquired about staying with Herman for a few months. This turned out to be Claus Johnson. Later this gentleman became his brother-in-law when he married his sister, Ester.

Throughout the course of the next few years Herman lived in various places and worked on different farms. For a time he even resided with his sister, Ruth, in McKinney.

Many farmers in the area were seeking good help and Herman jumped at the chance for steady work. He assisted Joe Knutson who lived on the farm close to his father's homestead. Knutson lived on the banks of the Mouse River and worked some of the richest land of the area. Herman also helped on the Swenson farms of McKinney and near the Mouse River Park.

In the *Renville County Farmers Press,* the "McKinney Mumbles" relate, "Bob Alexander and Herman Sjöqvist are hauling ice to Tolley" (January 27, 1921). And then again, "Judd Peterman and Herman Sjöqvist were down from Prosperity township collecting the bounty on a number of wolves they had killed. The former had eight and the latter six. The bounty is $2.50 each" (June 22, 1922).

The newly married couple, Myrtle and Herman Sjöqvist

෨ DURING EARLY SPRING of 1930, Herman was living and working at the John Wherley farm in Grover township. He was assisting with the spring planting. He had been there for a while, but he didn't plan to stay for long. Herman had his eyes set on a young lady by the name of Myrtle M. Shortridge. She was 15 at the time and he was a dashing man of 33.

Mrs. Lilly Shortridge, Myrtle's mother, liked Herman and approved of the courtship even though he was over 18 years older. She felt Herman would offer her daughter the stability she needed. With persuasion in mind she made an offer to Herman. "If you plan to marry my daughter, I will give you my house to live in. Kenmare can be your home."

And so it was, on June 7, 1930 Herman and Myrtle ventured off to the courthouse of Ward County and were married by Judge William Murray. Their witnesses were Mrs. Jess Shortridge (Myrtle's mother) and Mrs. L.C. Murray. It was a simple ceremony and over quickly.

Life became less hectic for Herman when the young couple settled in Kenmare. To the back of the house ran an alley and across this alleyway Herman set up a shop. He repaired and fixed almost anything and everything. This became his source of income.

Two years later, another Lilly was added to the household with the birth of a daughter, born October 8, 1932. In order to keep the names of the two Lillys apart, Mrs. Shortridge was called Lilly and her granddaughter became known as Dolly. Herman couldn't have been more proud of his little girl.

On February 12, 1936 four years later a son was added to the family. Now their home was full of the hustle and bustle of a rambunctious little fellow. Duane was truly full of energy and constantly on the go.

In later years family and people of the community knew when Herman was coming. They'd usually see a black Model A or T. It was hard to tell

Herman and Dolly *(above)*, and Dolly at Grandma Shortridge's place *(left)*

which one it was because he had added a little wooden box to the back. Was it a pickup or a car? It didn't really matter. It purred as Herman motored all around the village of Kenmare with his dogs, tools, or groceries in the back end and Myrtle in the front seat. ∞

Duane and Myrtle

Myrtle and Herman Sjöqvist with a later vehicle in 1960

*"The cords of death entangled me, the
anguish of the grave came upon me;
I was overcome by trouble and sorrow.
Then I called on the name of the LORD:
'O LORD, save me!'"*

Psalm 116:3-4

A Baby Lost

1920 – 1936

It was 1920 and John Sjöqvist at the age of 22 felt like he had been independent and on his own for years. And he had been. He was only 13 in 1911 when his father Johan Alfred Sjöqvist had passed away.

John had been flung into the working world. It really didn't matter that he was a mere child himself. He was expected to assist in adding to the earnings for his family. At times in his young years all John wanted to do was to be a kid. He dreaded and even hated all the responsibility on his shoulders. Sometimes he'd procrastinate or deviate his homeward direction in an attempt to shirk off the heavy responsibility. It felt like it was just too much to bear.

Why did life have to be so hard? Why were times so difficult? Why couldn't he just have fun? These questions haunted him over and over.

As a teenager he watched as other young men his age acted like they didn't have a care in the world. They went out with their friends and enjoyed themselves while having a good time. They could carouse around together and act "foot-loose and fancy-free."

School was on the back-burner for John. He attended a few months in the winter. Whatever learning he could glean from this short period of time would have to carry him for a lifetime.

John found his escape in music. Whether it was a violin, harmonica, button accordion, or any other musical instrument he could borrow, he found ways to produce beautiful melodies. Music became his refuge during difficult times.

But he was a perfectionist when it came to music. John required nothing but the best of himself as he worked with a musical instrument. His first choice of all instruments, the violin, was the only one he ever owned as a child. All others were borrowed from friends and neighbors. Everything he played was by ear. He would hear a song someplace and go home to create the exact or an even better reproduction. He went into another world as he labored to bring it to fruition. He could harmonize or play solo. Sometimes his frustration got the best of him, but in the end he found the escape he needed.

John, about 9 years old

ॐ JOHN SJÖQVIST WAS BARELY 20 when he first saw Bernice Alexander with new eyes. He had known her for years, but now he viewed her through the eyes of a young man. He was falling in love.

Bernice Alexander was only 18 when she married John Sjöqvist. It was 1921. And so, John became an earnest bread winner of his own newly created family. This time the responsibility felt right and even good. He could do this!

On January 5, 1922 the very first Sjöqvist grandchild was born. John and Bernice became the proud parents of a baby girl. They named her Marie.

The family continued to live at McKinney. Time passed and they added to their family. Eunice, Norman, Mae, and Gordon were born. The children were healthy and happy little ones.

John was soon 38 years old and he worked hard in his blacksmith shop to provide for his family. Bernice was 33 and expecting another child.

When Bernice went into labor, both John and Bernice anticipated the end result to be shear happiness. They loved their children and one more would be another wonderful addition.

In November of 1936 the world stopped for this young couple.

Something happened. Something went terribly wrong and the baby died. Bernice was beside herself. She had carried this little baby to full term and now there was no baby to love and coo over. Her husband could give her little comfort. He was totally devastated.

John left the house and entered his shop with one sole purpose in mind. He needed to do something with his hands. He would make something. Anything!

Tears streamed down his face as he sat and then paced around the shop. What could he do? It was then and there that he decided to shape a box that would hold his newborn baby. He would smooth and plane it for his little wee one that now lay so quiet and still.

John with daughter Marie and baby

With the most tender love possible, John fashioned a small box. He got out his tools and located the best wood possible. He wanted to create something perfect. Tears continued to fall as he planed the wood smooth and fastened the sides together. Bernice found him a piece of soft white material. He used this to line the little box. Working with his hands was therapeutic in dealing with his intense grief.

When the little box was completed John felt some relief. He set his tools aside and slowly walked into the house. John found his wife's sad eyes as he walked to her bedside. He needed help.

Taking his two oldest children aside, John asked if they would like to assist in preparing the little one. Big sisters, Marie and Eunice, were eager to help. They found clothes, dressed, wrapped, and laid the tiny baby into the beautiful tiny box.

John's family: Marie, Norman, Mae, Bernice, Gordon and Eunice

It was a very cool day in November when the family gathered to lay their little one to rest. Their hearts were heavy and matched the gloomy, overcast day. The graveside service was short. There was no eulogy telling of the many accomplishments of a long-lived life. The pastor read a few scripture passages and ended with a prayer. John and his family left the McKinney Cemetery slowly and quietly. There were no words uttered between them. Each brother, sister, mother, and father handled their grief in their own private way, but they had a common desire to return to the warmth and comfort of their own home. ∾

John and Bernice (1950s)

John, later in life

If you venture to the McKinney Cemetery and come to a stone that is carved with the words, "Baby Sjoquist - Nov. 1936". You have found the resting place of this little one that now resides in the arms of Jesus.

*"Many waters cannot quench love;
rivers cannot wash it away. If one
were to give all the wealth of his house
for love, it would be utterly scorned."*
Song of Songs 8:7

But, He's Not Swede!

1911...

Ingeborg Ragnhild
Eleonora Sjöqvist,
about 20 years old

For many years Ingeborg was the only girl in the Sjöqvist household in North Dakota. She did have an older sister in Sweden, but she often found it difficult to even remember what she looked like.

Ingeborg was tall for her age and quick on her feet. Often her two older brothers tried to dominate her. On most occasions Ingeborg could hold her own and stand up to the teasing and bossing from Herman and John.

Ingeborg loved the outdoors. She prided herself in knowing where every juneberry bush and every chokecherry tree grew. It was never work, but play in action when her Mor sent her out to glean the fruit from the coulees north of the home place.

She had a great love for animals and thoroughly enjoyed growing up on a farm. All the animals recognized her when Ingeborg approached the shed or pasture. She especially loved the horses and learned to ride at a very early age. She could break-in a young horse for riding by sheer determination and grit.

When her father died, Ingeborg was only ten years old. This event impacted her life in many ways. The most significant was the need for this young, lanky girl to be thrust into an adult world with adult responsibilities and expectations. She, along with her older brothers, needed to become wage earners. They were also expected to harvest the home crops the year of their father's death.

On April 18, 1915 two weeks after her little brother Edwin had passed away and one month after Ester and Erik's arrival, Ingeborg was confirmed in the Swedish Lutheran Church of Tolley, North Dakota. She was in a class with twelve other young people. Ten girls and three boys had studied and been taught entirely in the Swedish language. She was not quite 14 years old, but she felt a lot older. Ingeborg took her vows very seriously as she stood before the congregation and pledged to keep the faith. She had no intentions of falling away from the beliefs she held so dear.

In the fall of that same year, 1915, young Ingeborg followed the harvest crew. Being in the cook car was hard work. It encompassed many hours of hot labor to make all the meals and lunches for the hired hands. Each morning started long before sunup and ended long after sundown. *The Tolley Journal* reported on November 12, 1915, "Ingeborg Sjöqvist returned home from the cook car last week." She was 14 years old.

Doing domestic work was another way for her to bring home needed cash. She worked at the Wherley, John Morris, and Swenson homes, as well as many others. For a while she assisted a local seamstress. The experience served her well. Later in life she was known to cut fabric without the need of a pattern to make clothes for her family. Sometimes the work was for a day or two, a month or more, a season, or even long term. No labor job was too difficult for this young lady if she could take the earnings home to her Mor.

One summer day, Ingeborg met Ray Atwood. He was a hired hand and they were both employed by the Swenson family. It was an extremely hot, dry day when Ray came to the farm house. He knocked on the kitchen screen door and asked for Ingeborg.

When she came to the door with flour all over her hands. She stifled her bewilderment when he stated that he had forgotten his coat. When he brought it from the hall coat hook, Ingeborg couldn't believe it. It was a heavy winter overcoat!

Ray and Ingeborg's wedding photo, June 27, 1925, wearing clothes from the photography studio

Later, Ingeborg laughed, "It must be love! He certainly didn't need that heavy coat on such a blistering hot day!"

When her family heard about Ingeborg's thoughts of marriage, the only comment she heard voiced over and over was, "Well, we like Ray, but he's not Swede!"

Her retort was always the same, "Oh, yes! He's sweet!!"

On Saturday, June 27, 1925, Ingeborg and Ray Atwood were married at the Trinity Lutheran Church parsonage in Tolley, North Dakota. Their witnesses were Erik and Herman Sjöqvist, Ruth Sjöqvist, and Elda Conrad (a 13- or 14-year-old friend).

During the fall of 1925 Ray worked in the Theodore Mattson coal mine, west of Tolley. Ingeborg spent her days shocking grain for farmers.

This couple only lived in two places their entire married life. The first was a house west of the McKinney cemetery. It sat above the valley on a hill. It really wasn't much of a house. Numerous holes let the frigid winter air pour into the little abode. Ingeborg and Ray stuffed the holes with old rags and covered the gaps by nailing on flattened tin cans. They searched for ways to stay warm. Despite all the faults this house had, it was home.

Within a year Ray had struck a deal to rent one quarter of land from Gust Hendrickson. Gust lived in Grover township about two miles east of the original Sjöqvist homestead. Gust was a bachelor and needed help. As time passed, Gust became the missing Grandpa in the lives of the Atwood children. This man was kept busy!

Ray and Ingeborg had nine children, five boys and four girls. Gust got to know the first five before his death in 1935.

YEARS LATER, INGEBORG was honored with a distinction she deserved by receiving the Renville County Hall of Fame Award in 1965. Each year only one man and one woman was recognized for their pioneer contributions.

When called to the front to receive the award, Ingeborg recognized her husband Ray. "This one is for you. I couldn't have done any of this without Ray." ∽

Ingeborg (Sjöqvist) Atwood

Picture that hangs in the Renville County Courthouse Hall of Fame

Ray and Ingeborg Atwood's family, June 25, 1950: Glee and Jerry *(back)*; Dale, Eileen, June, and Justin *(middle)*; Raymond, Ray, Larry, Ingeborg, and Lela *(front)*

"For as high as the heavens are above the earth, so great is His love for those who fear Him, as far as the east is from the west, so far has He removed our transgressions from us."

Psalm 103:11-12

An Upright Man

1921...

After Erik's arrival in 1915 to North Dakota, *The Tolley Journal* reported the very next year this 12-year-old Swedish lad suffered the mishap of a broken arm. He was in the Kenmare Hospital. For the most part he appeared healthy until 1921 when he was admitted to the Tolley Hospital for reasons unknown.

In 1922 he worked in the blacksmith shop he owned in Greene, North Dakota. This little settlement was southwest of McKinney on the Mouse River. He did auto repairs, horseshoeing, and general blacksmithing. Owning his own blacksmith shop meant that income fluctuated and depended on the needs and seasons of the farmers who tilled the soil.

SJOQUIST GARAGE
Automobile repairing horseshoeing, general blacksmithing.—E. K. Sjoquist, Manager, Greene, N. D. 6-8p

Erik's blacksmithing ad, *Renville County Farmers Press,* December 28, 1922

Erik did this work until 1925 when he moved to the Thor Huly farm in Brandon Township. Now he was in the second township east of McKinney and the place of the county seat. He worked for Mr. Huly as a common farm laborer. There was always something to fix on a farm and Erik was kept extremely busy.

Years flew by. During the late 1930s and early 1940s World War II had started. Young men were lining up to enlist and leaving for far-off lands. Young women and men were in great demand for work in the defense plants on the West coast. The lure and appeal for American youth to assist our country was strong and electrifying. Jobs were created overnight, pulling people to California. Every line of work was available. No experience was required. People were trained on the jobsite.

Erik jumped at the chance for steady work. He yearned for a good reliable income. Not his former hit-or-miss earnings. And so, he left for the new frontiers of the West.

In California Erik found work in the shipyards. He was strong and willing to do whatever task lay before him. Supervisors appreciated his great work ethics. In time he became known as a very capable shipyard welder.

   WHILE LIVING IN CALIFORNIA, Erik met a tiny little gal named Isadore C. Wilson who was born in Logan, Iowa; raised in Nebraska; and attended Wayne State in Wayne, Nebraska. Eric was tall at six-feet-three inches. Isadore barely came midway between his waist and shoulder at a mere five feet. She was a teacher working with special education students.

Erik came to love her deeply with giant admiration and respect. Erik's easy going and laid back nature complimented Isadore's high energy and eager zest for life. In time they married and came to live in Hawthorne, California. Isadore continued to teach school and eventually Erik opened his own welding shop.

Isadore adored her "Erek" (Air-ek) as she called him. Everyone else called him "Erik" (Ear-ick).

Isadore and Erik Sjöqvist (November 18, 1964)

Isadore's students knew her husband as a friend and another teacher. Erik frequently met his wife for lunch. The students eagerly waited for Mr. Sjöqvist to play with them on the playground and visit with them over lunch. "It always seemed like the most challenging students related to him the best," Isadore often stated with pride.

But Erik's involvement didn't stop on the playground. He would attend classes at the local university with his wife. Isadore was taking graduate classes. Her professors were amazed with Erik's insight to the educational needs of her students. They were in disbelief that he had such a limited

Erik repairing cars

school background. How could he be so wise with only an eighth-grade education? He did all the requirements of the graduate classes, never reaping a grade or accreditation. What he did receive was the respect and admiration of everyone involved.

Erik and Isadore bought a small house at 15248 Del Rey Drive in Victorville, California. It wasn't long before it was filled with books and other school supplies for Isadore's teaching. They never had children of their own, but were abundantly rich in the children at Isadore's school. ∞

Cars advertising Erik & Claus Repair Shops (1940s)

Erik Sjöqvist with Dale Atwood (1946)

Isadore Sjöqvist and
Ingeborg Atwood
(April 1973)

Selma with Erik's car

"How beautiful you are, my darling! Oh, how beautiful!"

"My lover is radiant and ruddy, outstanding among ten thousand. His head is purest gold; his hair is wavy and black as a raven."

Song of Songs 1:15 and 5:10

A Grand Wedding

1945 – 1946

Ruth Sjöqvist and Johanna Servold, her neighbor friend, worked many years in the cookcar throughout the harvest time in North Dakota. This meant lots of traveling and even more hard labor and intensive work from before sunup until after sundown. It was not for the weak or those desiring a "good" time. It was bone tiring.

ॐ   NORTH DAKOTA HARVEST in the 1940s was a frenzy and flurry of activity. It was imperative to get the crop harvested before rain, hail, or snow descended on the fields. Hard work was the order of the day. A normal starting time was four or five in the morning. The end of the day was when darkness prevented work from being completed safely.

Prior to threshing, the grain needed to be cut and shocked. Bundles were made by a binder. One man would sit on a seat near the right side of the binder as he drove the horses down the grain field. The binder would cut, bundle with one string of twine, and drop the fresh grain bundle onto the stubble. Following behind the binder, a crew would shock the bundles. Two bundles were leaned together with the kernels up. More bundles were added to the sides and one bundle was placed on top to seal off possible rain.

The threshing machine was the heart and center of the harvest. It was a bundle eating monster. Horses pulling hayracks were driven down the rows of shocked bundles of grain. Men would throw the bundles onto the back of the wooden hayrack with pitchforks and then drive to the side of the thresher. Once in position, two men would throw the bundles rhythmically into the monster eating jaws. The shafts of grain would enter the machine. Inside the chaff was separated from the grain and the kernels tumbled out of a spout on the far right side. The chaff was blown out the back through a tall spout to create a giant straw pile.

The whole operation was run by a series of belts turned by a steam engine or tractor. A long giant belt connected the tractor to the thresher. It also allowed the tractor to remain a distance back from where the bundles were thrown and the grain extracted.

The noise was deafening with giant sounds coming from the tractor, threshing machine, belts, and pulleys. It was dusty and dirty from the straw chaff, grain dust, and smoke from the steam engine.

In the midst of this organized mayhem a small wooden house sat up on large iron wheels. It was positioned off to one side and was called the cook car. Sometimes a small tent was staked nearby for the women to sleep. In other cook cars cots folded down from the wall. Water crocks and other wooden storage boxes were removed from the interior and put under the cook car. A washstand sat close by for easy clean up by the men prior to eating.

Young women were hired to follow the harvest as it went from farm to farm. Their job was to provide three hardy meals and lunches both in the mid-morning and mid-afternoon. In order to accomplish all the work the women started their day at approximately four in the morning. By the time cleanup was accomplished and the bread was set for the following day, it

Inside a cook car *(Prairie Village Museum, Rugby, ND)*

might be eleven or twelve at night. The cook car was no romantic place to reside. It was hot with the cook stove fired up all day long. Little air moved through the small building. It was stifling!

Before the threshers would arouse, the women would be hard at work. The dough that had been set the night before was popped into the oven for fresh bread

Johanna Servold and Ruth outside the cook car (early 1940s)

for breakfast. The morning meal might consist of bread, pancakes, bacon, eggs, coffee, and more. The mid-morning and mid-afternoon lunches were usually sent out to the field with the water boys. These included sandwiches, cookies, and other easy to transport items.

A cook stove took up a large part of the cook car, but was an absolute necessity for all the baking. Fresh meat, milk, and eggs were purchased daily from farmers or in nearby towns. Life was a whirlwind and everything had to be on schedule.

When the harvest was completed on one farm, everything was packed and moved down the road to the next waiting farm. And so, the crew, machinery, horses, and cook car girls worked hard to accomplish a gigantic task. The harvest could last three to five months. Every farmer waited, holding their breath that the threshing crew would arrive in time and all would go well. They prayed that their earnings for an entire year would be brought in safely, quickly, and in sufficient abundance.

℘ RUTH AND JOHANNA ENJOYED a friendship that grew into a deep love and understanding. They were both good cooks and the food they made brought smiles to the grubby, dirty farm hands. The men appreciated the great taste of good home cooking.

Dinner and supper needed to be hearty with meat and potatoes. Besides the main courses Ruth and Johanna made pies, cakes, and cookies for the satisfaction of those having a sweet tooth. The men seldom turned down these precious delicacies. They were always hungry after doing many hours of hard physical labor out in the hot, hot sun.

"We have to give them solid food in order to hold their feet on the ground," Johanna would comment.

Ruth would laugh and add, "We sure don't want to be responsible for them shriveling up and blowing away in this Dakota wind."

The two gals laughed a lot through their labors. They enjoyed each other's company and their conversations were deep and intense. Many times they discussed their families and what was going on "back home." They missed their loved ones and always felt a strong tug in that direction.

Ruth and Johanna got their share of attention from all the men folk surrounding them. As women, they were a rare commodity in a sea of male domination. For the most part the men were respectful and kind. They kept their distance with limited communication with the girls. They did grunt "*Tack*" upon completion of the meal. One day a new gentleman joined the crew. He came from Iowa, but had originally grown up in Nebraska. His name was Virgil Olson.

Virgil was an extremely hard worker. He also had a winsome smile and a way about him with the other men on the crew. He was sensitive to their needs and could engage even the quietest man in a conversation. He had a great sense of humor and made everyone laugh with his stories and jokes. People enjoyed being around him.

Both Ruth and Johanna noticed Virgil the day he joined the threshing crew. Behind the scenes they'd laugh at his antics. Sometimes they caught themselves laughing aloud at his numerous jokes.

Virgil was captivating to say the least! His full head of dark hair added to an already handsome look.

Ruth fell for him hook, line, and sinker. Johanna once caught her ready to put a cup of salt instead of a cup of sugar into a pie being prepared. "Whew, I caught you in time!" she remarked.

Johanna had to work hard to keep her friend's feet on the ground and her head out of the clouds. Ruth may have been 40 years old, but she was smitten.

Somehow Ruth and Virgil managed to spend time together. During this season of hard work they'd usually talk late into the night after the work was done. Through these conversations they both found they had many things in common.

Even though they had numerous friends, they were both lonely and in search of a lifelong companion. They also shared a deep faith in God and a love for their families.

When Virgil proposed to Ruth, she readily agreed. She was eager to be married and begin a new life with this man she loved. On April 28, 1946 Ruth Josefina Helena Sjöqvist and Virgil Cyrus Olson were married by Pastor G. Gunsten in the Lutheran Church at Montpelier, North Dakota.

Ruth's sister and her husband, Ester and Claus Johnson, were their witnesses. Johanna Servold and Ruth's niece, June Atwood, were her other attendants. Virgil's attendants were Ruth's brother, Erik Sjöqvist, and her nephew, Edwin Johnson. The ring bearer was Raymond Atwood. He wore a white sailor suit and carried the ring pillow. The neighbor girl and Lela Atwood were flower girls and wore pale yellow dresses. These two little girls carried flowers and picked the petals off, slowly dropping them on the aisle as they walked to the front of the church.

It was an extremely windy day as the wedding party posed for pictures on the front steps. Everyone remembered the wind blowing their hair into their eyes. The children could hardly wait for this part of the wedding process to be over.

Ruth had been living with her mother, Selma, in Ypsilanti, North Dakota. And so, Virgil joined them in the large farmhouse they all shared.

The two newlyweds were no young kids. Ruth was 40 and Virgil was 46, but they were definitely in love. It was a happy day for all!! ∽

Back Row: Ray Atwood, Claus Johnson, Ester Johnson, Erik Sjöqvist, Edwin Johnson
Middle Row: Virgil Olson, Ruth Olson, Johanna Servold, June Atwood
Front Row: Raymond Atwood, neighbor girl, Lela Atwood

Flower girl, Lela Atwood

Sjöqvist Children as Adults

Ester and Claus Johnson, 1950s

Myrtle and Herman Sjoquist, 1960

John and Bernice Sjoquist, 1965

Ray and Ingeborg Atwood, 1965

Isadore and Erik Sjoqvist, 1963

Virgil and Ruth Olson, 1946

"I have fought the good fight,
I have finished the race,
I have kept the faith."

2 Timothy 4:7

Epilogue

Selma Amanda
Dahlgren Sjöqvist
(mid 1940s)

Selma Amanda Dahlgren Sjöqvist lived the rest of her life in Lawndale, California with her youngest daughter, Ruth Olson. She never walked again after breaking her hip, however, she remained in good health otherwise. Until her dying day, she loved watching wrestling and "American Bandstand" on television.

On August 21, 1961 Selma passed away at the grand old age of 91. She outlived her husband, Johan, and two of her seven children. Edwin, her youngest child, died in 1915 and her oldest daughter Ester in 1954. Two son-in-laws had also passed away; Claus Johnson (Ester's husband) in 1957 and Virgil Olson (Ruth's husband) in 1960.

Selma left a true legacy of 17 grandchildren, countless great grandchildren, and many great, great grandchildren.

But, above all, Selma Amanda Dahlgren Sjöqvist left us an example of life lived in the Faith. She believed troubles come to everyone, but that is when you grab hold of God's hand and hang on tight. She knew it was the only way to get through the trials life brought her way. These trials led to greater blessings and helped her to remain focused as she looked forward to heaven. ∽

APPENDIX

Threshing machine

Acknowledgments

To my children, brothers, sisters, extended family and friends who brought me pictures, advised me, and listened to me expound and share the stories. You are appreciated more than you will ever know. My heart is filled with love for all of you! I want to thank my grandparents and parents for making this possible and my children for making it necessary.

Many thanks! *Många Tack!!*

Lela S. Peterson

Lela Selma Atwood Peterson

182

Timeline of Events

Year	Sjöqvist Family	Worldwide Happenings
1895	Selma Amanda Dahlgren marries Johan Alfred Sjöqvist	*Alfred Nobel, who was born in Sweden, establishes the Nobel prize
1901	Ingeborg Sjöqvist is born	*Oil discovered in Texas *President McKinley killed; Theodore Roosevelt becomes 26th President
1903	Johan Sjöqvist leaves for America	*1st baseball World Series *Panama gains independence *Ford Motor Company and Pepsi Cola formed *Due to drought the Niagara US Falls runs short of water
1904	Selma Sjöqvist comes to North Dakota with 3 of their 5 children	*Ice cream cone makes debut *Wright brothers take flight *US buys Panama for $10 million
1908	Johan, Selma & children become US naturalized citizens	*Lusitania crosses Atlantic in 4 days and 15 hours *1st Ford Model T built
1909	Johan gains the homestead rights	*Taft inaugurated as US president during 10-inch snowfall *Peary & Henson reach North pole
1911	Johan Sjöqvist dies	*ND enacts a hail insurance law *1st auto race at Indianapolis *Amundsen reaches South pole
1912	Selma obtains $100 loan	*Titanic sank after hitting an iceberg on April 15

1915	Ester & Erik come to America, Edwin Sjöqvist dies	*Lusitania sunk; 1,198 lives lost *Babe Ruth enters baseball *Girls Scouts founded *Ford makes one-millionth Model T *Woodrow Wilson is US president
1918	Sjöqvist homestead foreclosure sale in Mohall, ND	*Civil War in Finland *Spanish influenza worldwide; 21,000 die in one week in US *Daylight savings time first used *World War I ends on November 11
1920	Selma moves from homestead to McKinney	*League of Nations formed *Panama Canal opens *19th Amendment ratified (women's suffrage) *Nobel Prize to President Wilson *Bob Hope becomes citizen
1935 / 1936	Selma moves to Montpelier, ND; Government takes river land - 22,000 acres to create the Upper Souris Wildlife Game Refuge and Preserve	*Iceland 1st to legalize abortion *Hitler rearms Germany *Fibber McGee & Molly air on radio *Babe Ruth retires from baseball *FDR becomes president *German Jews deprived of citizenship *Stalin (Russia) & Mussolini (Italy) in power
1946	Selma's youngest daughter, Ruth, marries Virgil Olson	*Roosevelt dime 1st issued *Truman is President *US patent filed for H-bomb *Nuremberg Nazi trials find 22 guilty of war crimes
1961	Selma Sjöqvist passes away on August 21 at 91+ years	*US/Cuba break relationships *President Kennedy creates Peace Corp *Beatles & Elvis – popular music *MN Vikings football formed *Freedom Riders board buses *Martin Luther King works for civil rights

Johan Alfred Sjöqvist

Born - April 4, 1869
in Madesjö, Sweden (Småland/Kalmar).

Parents – married November 3, 1868;
farmers in Tjukehall, Sweden.

Frans Peter Olsson Sjögren
    born December 9, 1838 in Madesjö,
    died January 18, 1901 in Madesjö.

Christina Petersdotter Sjögren
    born December 3, 1837 in Kristvalla,
    died March 24, 1908 in Madesjö.

Siblings - He was the oldest of six children (4 boys and 2 girls), and the only one to marry and have children. Upon his death in 1911 there remained only one sister, Alma, who was injured and walked with a limp; she died December 5, 1966.

Married - He was just shy of 26 years old when he married Selma Amanda Dahlgren on February 19, 1895 in Madesjö.

Characteristics - Height - 6 feet 2 inches; Eyes - blue; Hair - brown.

Immigrated to the United States - Left Madesjö on March 13, 1903 and Göteborg,

Sweden on March 22, 1903. From Liverpool, England he departed on the vessel *Saxonia* on March 24, 1903. Arrived in Boston Port on April 3, 1903 with $10. He came by railroad through Canada to Kenmare, ND on April 7, 1903.

Occupations - shoemaker in Sweden; farmer in North Dakota.

Homesteaded in Grover – Township 162, Range 86, Section 28; West half of NE quarter, East half of NW quarter.

Citizenship & Naturalization - First Papers filed on July 6, 1903 in Ward County, Eighth Judicial District, North Dakota (Grover township was a part of Ward County at that time. Later this area became a part of Renville County). Second Papers applied for on June 19, 1908. Aaron A. Johnson and Joseph Knudson were witnesses to final petition. Certification rendered for Johan, Selma and all seven children (including two in Sweden) on October 2, 1908.

"Secured" the homestead on May 27, 1909 when William H. Taft was President of the United States for a cost of fees totaling $5.25.

Children - Ester, Herman, John, Ingeborg, Erik, Ruth, Edwin.

Death - October 3, 1911 at 2 am in Grover, North Dakota (42 years, 5 months, 29 days old), attended to by Dr. S. Rainville.

Burial - McKinney Cemetery, Swedish Lutheran Church, Tolley, ND.

Selma Amanda Dahlgren Sjöqvist

Born - April 25, 1870 in Madesjö, Sweden (Småland/Kalmar).

Parents - married October 7, 1868.

Johan Dahlgren
   born June 4, 1829 in Halleberga,
   died January 8, 1914 in Madesjö.

Maria Helena Jonsson Dahlgren
   born July 7, 1831 in Madesjö,
   died October 3, 1913 in Madesjö.

Siblings – None; she was an only child.

Married - She was nearly 25 years old when married to Johan Alfred Sjöqvist on February 19, 1895 in the parish of Madesjö, Sweden. Resided in Gränö in Kalmar Län, Sweden.

Children - (three daughters and four sons) Ester, Herman, John, Ingeborg, Erik, Ruth, Edwin.

Occupation - Housewife.

Immigrated to the United States - on the vessel *Saxonia*. Carl Jonson (Johnson) came from Grover township to escort Selma and three children. Left Madesjö on October 18, 1904 with children, Herman (age about 8), John (age 6), and Ingeborg (age 3). Leaving behind - Ester (age about 9) and Erik (age 1) in Sweden with her parents, Johan and Maria Dahlgren. Arrived in Boston on November 2, 1904 and on to Estevan, Saskatchewan with $20 in cash and passage paid by Carl Jonson/Johnson.

US Census - **1910**, Johan & Selma reside in Grover with five of seven children. **1920**, Selma resides in Grover with six children (Edwin has died). **1930**, Selma resides in McKinney with Erik (26) and Ruth (24). **1940**, Selma resides in Montpelier, Stutsman County, North Dakota with Erik (36) and Ruth (34).

Relocations - National Wildlife Refuge claimed 22,000 acres along the Mouse River including land two miles north of the Mouse River Park and south through all of Renville County and into Ward County with a large dam constructed at the countyline in 1935-1936. This included all of McKinney where she was residing. It is believed Selma left in (approximately) 1936.

Moved to Ypsilanti, North Dakota (Near Montpelier, ND) and lived with Ruth and Erik.

Left North Dakota and moved to California with (daughter) Ruth and Virgil Olson at 4514 West 171 Street; Lawndale, California 90260 until her death.

Death - August 21, 1961 at the age of 91 years, 3 months, and 28 days.

Burial - Inglewood Park Cemetery (Los Angeles County), Plot: Lot 811 Section: Avalon; 720 E. Florence Avenue, Inglewood, California.

Note: Error on tombstone "SELMA S. JOQVIST"

Ester Gunhild Alfrida Sjöqvist Johnson

Born - December 1, 1895 in Madesjö, Sweden.

Immigrated to the US - Ester stayed in Sweden when her father and mother left for America and lived with grandparents on mother's side, Johan & Maria Dahlgren. She left Göteborg, Sweden on February 8, 1915 by train for Bergen, Norway. Sailed to America on February 11, 1915 from Bergen, Hordaland, Norway on the *S. S. Kristianiafjord*. Arrived in New York at Ellis Island on February 20, 1915. She was 19 years old and came with her brother, Erik, age 11 years. Her last place of residency was Algustboda, Sweden. She had $1 in her possession, was 5 feet 9 inches in height and had brown hair and blue eyes. Upon arrival at Ellis Island she was admitted to the hospital and after 19 days was discharged. Arrived by railway at the home of her mother, Selma, in Grover, ND on March 15, 1915.

Work - Hultqvist home in Algustboda, Sweden. Domestic work at the homes of Joseph Knudson, Nels Kvales, and many others in the Grover and McKinney area.

Married - Claus (Claude) Johnson in Hardisty, Alberta, Canada on May 7, 1921.

Husband - Claus (Klas/Claude) Johnson. Born on June 5, 1892 in Istorp, Sweden. Immigrated to Quebec, Canada in 1913 from Istorp, Västergötland, Sweden. Census, 1916 - living in Battle River, Alberta, Canada. Census, 1921 - living in Hughenden, Alberta. Moved to McKinney, ND on December 17, 1921 on the Canadian Pacific Railway.

Child - Edwin Johan was born February 4, 1922 in McKinney, ND; married on July 14, 1946 to Edna Mae Podoll (born October 12, 1925 in Nortonville, ND), and died on December 26, 1998 at Riverside, California. (Edna died on May 6, 2008 at Riverside, California.)

Grandchildren - Sherry, Jeffrey, and Claudia Johnson.

US Census - **1920**, with Selma in Grover Township, North Dakota. **1930**, with Claus and son, Edwin, in Grover Township, North Dakota. **1940**, on a rented farm in Stutsman County, Manns Township in North Dakota.

Relocations - Moved to California in the late 1940s.

Death - Ester died April 6, 1954 at the age of 58 years, 4 months, 5 days. Claus died February 15, 1957 at the age of 64 years, 8 months, 10 days.

Burial - Roosevelt Memorial Park (Lots 1 & 2 of Section 4205); 18255 S. Vermont Avenue, Gardena, California.

Herman Gunnar Emanuel Sjöqvist

Born - November 14, 1896 in Madesjö, Sweden.

Immigrated to the United States - on the vessel *Saxonia*. Left Madesjö on October 18, 1904 at age 8 with mother, Selma, and brother, John (6), and sister, Ingeborg (3). Arrived in Boston port on November 2, 1904 and by railway to Estevan, Saskatchewan, Canada and then Grover township.

Dad's death - October 3, 1911, six weeks before Herman's 15th birthday.

Confirmation - March 31, 1912, age 15, with brother John. Swedish Lutheran Church, Tolley, ND.

Military - inducted at Mohall on August 28, 1918. Sent to Camp Lewis, Washington. Served in 166th Depot Brigade, to Sept Company M, lst Infantry. World War I ended on November 11, 1918. Discharged January 25, 1919 at Camp Lewis as a Private.

Census - **1920**, lived with mother, Selma, at Grover, North Dakota. **1925**, lived with sister, Ruth, in McKinney, North Dakota. **1930**, lived and worked at the John J. Wherley farm in Grover Township, North Dakota. **1940**, lived in Ward County at Kenmare, North Dakota.

Work in North Dakota - Wilbur Johnson, hauling hay; Joseph Knudson farm; John Wherley farm; Hauled ice with Bob Alexander; Hunted wolves with Judd Peterman; Hauled wood; Swenson farms as a laborer.

Married - At nearly age 35, Herman married Myrtle M. Shortridge (age 15, born February 17, 1915) on June 7, 1930 in the Ward County courthouse by Judge William Murray. Witnesses: Mrs. Jess(ie) Shortridge (mother) and Mrs. Elsie Murray (Judge's wife).

Children
Lilly "Dolly", born October 8, 1932 and
   died April 30, 1990.
Duane, born February 12, 1936 and
   died April 19, 2013.

Death - Herman died February 16, 1969 in Tolley, North Dakota; Myrtle died April 3, 1966 in Kenmare, North Dakota.

Burial - Kenmare, North Dakota, Lakeview Cemetery (west of town), Nazareth Lutheran Church, Kenmare, ND.

Note: There are discrepancies on the two tombstones. The one on the left should read World War I (not World War II) and birth date of November 14, 1896 (not 1895).

John Ragnar Julius Sjöqvist

Born - June 16, 1898 in Madesjö, Sweden.

Immigrated to the United States - on the vessel *Saxonia*. Left Madesjö on October 18, 1904 at age 6 with mother, Selma, and brother, Herman (8), and sister Ingeborg (3). Arrived in Boston port on November 2, 1904 and on to Estevan, Saskatchewan, Canada by railway and then to Grover township.

Dad's death - October 3, 1911, when John was 13 years old.

Confirmation - March 31, 1912, age of 13 years and 9 months with brother Herman at the Swedish Lutheran Church, Tolley, ND.

Work - Wilbur Johnson with chores; Grover farmers; Brandon Township farms; Swenson farms in McKinney; Owned his own blacksmith shop in Tolley, ND.

Vehicles - on November 10, 1916 owned a Ford car. On November 17, 1916 in *The Tolley Journal*: "Something that resembled a 1917 model was seen going along the river last Monday, when John Sjöquist hauled his Ford home with a team after the recent snow."

Military - registered card completed on September 12, 1918 at the age of 20; never drafted.

Census - **1920**, living with mother, Selma, in Grover Township, North Dakota. **1930**, married and living in McKinney with wife Bernice and 3 children. **1940**, living in Tolley, North Dakota, Renville County with wife Bernice who was doing WPA sewing for income.

Marriage - April 25, 1921, at the age of 22 to Bernice M. Alexander, age 18 (born February 27, 1903).

Children

Marie A.: born January 5, 1922; married Leslie Koran; died February 22, 1984 in California.

Eunice: born October 12, 1925; married Edward Zeltinger/Krueger; died June 17, 2003 in North Dakota.

Norman John: born April 9, 1928; married Bertha Shipman; died October 10, 1984 in California.

Mae: born May 22, 1930; married Lawrence Ethan; died February 8, 2000 in North Dakota.

Gordon D.: born April 14, 1932; married Rose Mueller; died March 15, 1990 in Tolley, North Dakota.

Baby: born & died 1936 in Tolley, North Dakota.

Death - August 8, 1970 (John), Tolley, North Dakota. November 5, 1969 (Bernice), Tolley, North Dakota.

Burial - Both at McKinney Cemetary, Swedish Lutheran Church; August 12, 1970 (John); November 8, 1969 (Bernice).

Ingeborg Ragnhild Eleonora Sjöqvist Atwood

Born - July 12, 1901 in Madesjö, Sweden.

Baptized - July 15, 1901 by Minister Medelius in Madesjö.

Prayer of Thanksgiving (krykotagning) - August 18, 1901 (given by mother at church altar); also when mother was officially accepted back into the church after giving birth.

Immigrated to the United States - on the vessel *Saxonia*. Left Madesjö on October 18, 1904 at age 3 with mother, Selma, and brothers, Herman (8), and John (6). Arrived in Boston port on November 2, 1904 and on by railway to Estevan, Saskatchewan, Canada and then Grover, ND township.

Naturalized - on October 2, 1908 with the entire Sjöqvist family.

Dad's death - October 3, 1911, when Ingeborg was 10 years old.

Confirmation - Swedish Lutheran Church (in Swedish) on April 18, 1915 in a class of 13 (10 girls and 3 boys).

Work - Domestic worker on various farms in Grover & McKinney, North Dakota: The Swenson farms; John Wherley farm; Worked in the cook car for the threshing crew; Sewed clothes and other items with a seamstress in the area.

Census - **1910**, lived with mother and father on homestead in Grover. **1920**, lived with mother in Grover. **1930**, lived with husband and two children on Gus Hendrickson farm in Grover. **1940**, lived with husband and seven children on farm in Grover.

Married - June 27, 1925 - Trinity Lutheran Church parsonage. Husband, Raymond Donald Atwood, born March 8, 1895 in Alexandria, Minnesota. Witnesses - Erik & Herman Sjöqvist, Ruth Sjöqvist & Elda Conrad.

Church - became a member of Trinity Lutheran Church, Tolley, ND on Palm Sunday, April 18, 1943. (Prior to this they attended the Swedish Lutheran Church in Tolley, ND.)

Children

June Ruth: born June 3, 1926; married Albert Schmitz, June 27, 1948; died Oct. 24, 2014.

Justin Raymond: born Dec. 28, 1927; married Joyce Coughlin, Oct. 17, 1965; died November 19, 2000.

Dale Donovan: born June 27, 1930; married Arlis Irwin, August 24, 1958; died May 20, 2004.

Glee Ingeborg: born April 3, 1932; married Roger Grau, June 19, 1955.

Jerry Dean: born Dec. 21, 1934; married Charlotte Tennyson, Sept. 14, 1954; died March 12, 2005.

Eileen Elenor: born January 18, 1937; married Ernest Ward, March 2, 1958.

Raymond Erick: born May 2, 1939; married Shirley Anderson, June 8, 1963.

Lela Selma: born June 28, 1942; married Wayne Peterson, August 17, 1969.

Larry Lyman: born July 8, 1944; married Karen Havskjold, July 14, 1968.

Homes - Home in Gränö, Sweden. Raised on the North Dakota homestead in Grover township. Lived in a house on a west hill above McKinney Cemetery when first married. Lived rest of her life on the same farm in Grover Township, Tolley, ND.

House Fire - December 7, 1934 (two weeks prior to the birth of her son, Jerry). Entire house and belongings lost, except for June's doll and a suitcase.

Death - December 27, 1973 (Ingeborg), May 12, 1972 (Raymond).

Burial - Both Ingeborg and Raymond buried at McKinney Cemetery, Trinity Lutheran Church, Tolley, ND.

Erik Knut Valdemar Sjöqvist

Born - May 31, 1903 in Madesjö, Sweden to Johan and Selma Sjöqvist.

Stayed in Sweden - When his father (1903) and mother (1904) left for America, Erik stayed in Sweden and lived with maternal grandparents, Johan and Maria Dahlgren. Then lived with sister, Ester, in Algustboda, Sweden.

Immigrated to the US - Left Göteborg, Sweden on February 8, 1915 by train for Bergen, Norway. Sailed on February 11, 1915 from Bergen, Hordaland, Norway on the *S. S. Kristianiafjord*. Arrived in New York at Ellis Island on February 20, 1915. He was 11 years old and came with his sister, Ester, aged 19 years. His last place of residency in Sweden was Algustboda. He was 4 feet 7 inches with brown hair and blue eyes when he immigrated. He was able to stay with his sister the entire 19 days she was hospitalized upon arrival. They arrived at the home of his mother, Selma, in Grover township on March 15, 1915.

Confirmation - August 4, 1918 with his sister, Ruth, at The Evangelical (Swedish) Lutheran Church.

Worked - Farms in Grover, McKinney, and Hamlet in North Dakota. Owned his own repair shop/mechanic in Greene, ND (1922). Blacksmith in Ypsilanti, ND. Shipyard welder in California.

Census - **1920**, lived with mother in Grover, North Dakota. **1925**, lived and worked for Thor & Mary Huly and four children in Hamlet Township, North Dakota. **1930**, lived with mother and sister, Ruth, in McKinney, North Dakota. **1940**, lived with mother and sister, Ruth, in Montpelier, Stutsman County, ND.

Moved - from North Dakota to California in the 1940s. His last known address was 15248 Del Rey Dr., Victorville, California 92392.

Married - Isadore C. Wilson (born March 4, 1904 in Logan, Iowa). She attended college in Wayne, Nebraska and taught special education students.

Death - July 20, 1966 (Erik), Victorville, California. June 9, 1994 (Isadore), Issaquah, Washington (last residence).

Burial - Forest Lawn Memorial Park in Glendale, California (Los Angeles County); Plot: Eventide, Map 1, Lot 3434, Spaces 2 & 3 (both Erik and Isadore).

Note: There is no stone for Isadore.

Ruth Josefina Helena Sjöqvist Olson

Born - August 10, 1905 to Johan & Selma Sjöqvist of Grover Township (North Dakota).

Baptized - August 20, 1905.

Confirmation - August 4, 1918 with her brother Erik at The Evangelical (Swedish) Lutheran Church.

Worked - Domestic work at various farm homes in Grover and McKinney. Worked in a cookcar as she followed the threshing crew. Thread snipper in a California clothing factory.

Married - Virgil C. Olson (born January 10, 1900). Adopted son, originally from Stromsburg, Nebraska before coming to ND lived in Harlan, Iowa. Wedding on April 28, 1946 in the Lutheran Church by Pastor G. Gunsten in Montpelier, North Dakota.

Census - **1910**, with parents on homestead in Grover. **1920**, with mother in Grover. **1930**, with mother and brother, Erik, in McKinney. **1940**, lived with mother and brother, Erik, in Montpelier, Stutsman County, ND.

Moved - to California after 1946 marriage. Virgil worked for a construction crew (paved parking lot of The Glass Church by the ocean). Ruth stayed at home with mother. Later worked in dress/clothes making factory, snipping threads from sewn pieces.

Last known address - 4514 West 171 Street, Lawndale, California 90260.

Death - March 29, 1974 (Ruth); March 14, 1960 (Virgil).

Burial - Inglewood Park Cemetery (Los Angeles County); 720 E. Florence Avenue, Inglewood, California; Section: Avalon, Lots: 812 & 813.

Edwin Sigmund Herbert Sjöqvist

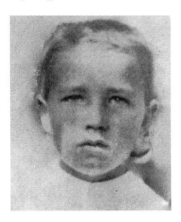

Born - May 6, 1907 in Grover, North Dakota.

School - Grover School #2, west of river, near Joe Knudson's farm.

Census - 1910, living with parents on homestead in Grover Township, North Dakota.

Illness - Lasted 28 days. Started as tonsillitis and affected kidneys, liver, and heart. Ended with pneumonia.

Death - April 22, 1915, five weeks after Ester and Erik arrived from Sweden; seven years, 11 months, 14 days.

Burial - Swedish Lutheran Church, McKinney Cemetery, North Dakota.

Dear Ancestor

AUTHOR UNKNOWN

Your tombstone stands among the rest;
  neglected and alone.
The name and date are chiseled out on
  polished marble stone.

It reaches out to all who care.
  It is too late to mourn.
You didn't know that I exist.
  You died and I was born.

Yet each of us are cells of you in flesh,
  in blood, in bone.
Our heart contracts and beats a pulse
  entirely not our own.

Dear ancestor, the place you filled
  One hundred years ago,
Spreads out among the ones you left
  Who would have loved you so.

I wonder if you lived and loved,
  I wonder if you knew
That someday I would find this spot,
  And come to visit you.

May All Who Come Behind Us Find Us Faithful

by Jon Mohr, 1987

We're pilgrims on the journey
Of the narrow road
And those who've gone before us line the way
Cheering on the faithful,
encouraging the weary
Their lives a stirring testament to God's sustaining grace

Surrounded by so great a cloud of witnesses
Let us run the race not only for the prize
But as those who've gone before us
Let us leave to those behind us
The heritage of faithfulness passed on through godly lives

Chorus:
Oh may all who come behind us find us faithful
May the fire of our devotion light their way
May the footprints that we leave
Lead them to believe
And the lives we live inspire them to obey
Oh may all who come behind us find us faithful

After all our hopes and dreams have come and gone
And our children sift through all we've left behind
May the clues that they discover and the memories they uncover
Become the light that leads them to the road we each must find

Chorus

My Resources

My sources of information include:

Visits and telephone calls with relatives and friends who entertained the many questions asked and shared numerous photos.

Family History Workshops in Moorhead, MN and Grand Forks, ND.

Visits and emails with friends from Sweden, and the archival records of Göteborg, Vadstena and Växjö, Sweden.

Trips to Sweden where I visited the places where Selma and her family lived, worshipped, and departed.

Cemeteries, old documents, old photos, obituaries, and church records.

The entire runnings of Tolley newspapers, from the North Dakota State Archives (microfilm) and the Renville County Farmer office (actual 100+ year old newspapers), plus photos from the *Kenmare News.*

Standard Atlas of Renville County North Dakota; Geo. A. Ogle & Co. Publishers, Chicago, 1914.

North Dakota State Archives, and various North Dakota county court house records. Libraries and librarians (including the University of North Dakota Special Collections).

Minnkota Genealogical Society for information, speakers, and encouragement.

Ellisisland.com, and telephone interview with Barry Mareno, librarian and historian of Ellis Island Library Research.

Ancestry.com

Findagrave.com

Familysearch.org

The Holy Bible, New International Version.

Countless books concerning immigration, naturalization, and homesteading.

Clemensson, Per, and Kjell Andersson. *Your Swedish Roots: A Step by Step Handbook.* Provo, UT: Ancestry, a division of MyFamily.com, Inc., 1983.

Weiss, Feri Felix. *The Sieve: Or Revelations of the Man Mill, being the truth about American Immigration.* Boston: The Page Company in Boston, 1921.

Hembree, Blanche. *Fate, Destiny, Necessity on Renville's Prairies.* N.p.: n.p, 1977.

Renville County Old Settler's Association. Renville County History, 1901 - 1976. N.p.: Renville County Old Settler's Association, 1976.

Stark, Louise, and Duane Stark. *Tolley, North Dakota and Surrounding Area, Forever Remembered: Centennial, 1905-2005.* Tolley, North Dakota: Tolley Centennial Committee, 2005.

Author Lela Peterson

Lela Selma Atwood Peterson knew very little of her mother's background other than the stories that her mother shared as they washed dishes, scrubbed floors, weeded the garden, or milked cows. Even though she relished the rare visits with her grandmother, it was never quite enough. She always had a deep yearning to learn more. And so, began her search. She traveled to Sweden to trace the very beginnings of Johan and Selma's journey. It was a great thrill for Lela to stand by the remains of the original Sjöqvist home. While in Sweden she delved into the archival records of Vadstena and Växjö.

Lela grew up in Grover township. Her parents and family lived about two and a quarter miles from the original Sjöqvist homestead. The entire family roamed those very same hills in search of the best juneberries. It was during this time she realized how much at home her mother was in this setting.

Lela is a graduate of both Minot State University and the University of North Dakota. For many years she taught elementary school in North Dakota, Wisconsin, and Germany. In her retirement she has enjoyed writing family history and genealogical research.

She resides in North Dakota and cares part time for her two grandchildren. In her spare time she enjoys traveling, gardening, reading, arts, and crafts.

Christmas 1950 on the farm in Grover Township, North Dakota

For Future Generations

Annika Lynn (5) and Jon Lawrence (3) look at the picture of their
mormors mormor and *mormors morfar* (great, great grandmother and
great, great grandfather), Selma and Johan Sjöqvist.
Their *mormor* wrote this story.
And so, the legacy continues!

*"For the Lord is the great God, the great King above
all gods. In his hand are the depths of the earth, and
mountain peaks belong to him. The sea is his, for he
made it, and his hands formed the dry land."*

Psalm 95:3-5

Made in the USA
Middletown, DE
30 November 2019

79655972R00118